MELCHIZEDEK
TRUTH PRINCIPLES

DEDICATION

Dedicated to George G. Price and George A. Greenlee—two souls devoted to the Eternal Principles of Truth.

MELCHIZEDEK
TRUTH PRINCIPLES

FROM THE
ANCIENT MYSTICAL WHITE BROTHERHOOD

Fourth DIMENSIONAL Teachings
Through
FRATER ACHAD

DeVorss & Co., *Publishers*
1641 Lincoln Boulevard
Santa Monica, Calif. 90404

Printed in the United States of America
DeVorss & Co., 1641 Lincoln Blvd., Santa Monica, Calif. 90404

ABOUT THE AUTHOR

FRATER ACHAD, in the present era of life, was a quiet, humble but engaging mystic, who soon won the love and respect of those who crossed his path. His name was George Graham Price. He aided many people with his clairvoyance and conscious counseling, but by far the bulk of his contribution to this world lies in the beautiful lessons that came through him in suspended mental animation.

The gentle graciousness with which he surrendered his body and his voice box to be used by the Ancient Mystical White Brotherhood is but a shadow to the Great Wisdom, the love and understanding warmth that is such an integral part of these lessons.

Many of the parables and paradoxes in our beloved Bible are made crystal clear in the interpretations given.

During the last six years of his life when he lived in our midst, such information and guidance were received that touched on many of the common and uncommon problems of life with constructive suggestions for grappling with them successfully.

—C. R.

ABOUT THE BOOK

SPIRITUALLY—YOU ARE A GIANT

Just as you find the laws of mathematics and the sciences are specific and provable, you find that the laws governing the mental and spiritual realms are also specific, provable and usable. They will work unfailingly for everyone who believes and applies them.

You, too, will absorb the beauty and benefits of these revealed truths which come to all who would take time to read, understand and apply them. Those who have studied these lessons untold times still thrill to their eternal Truth.

In our search beyond the self-consciousness of man into that cosmic realm of regenerated thinking, to really see with the eyes of God, we were blessed by the Light of Illumination which came to us through these visits from the Ancient Mystical White Brotherhood. They give the reader a new concept of the Universal Brotherhood of man and a much clearer understanding of how to apply with greater ease these mental and spiritual laws for positive good . . . TO KNOW THE TRUTHS THAT SET ONE FREE from the common confusion of today's world.

CONTENTS

PATHWAY OF THE SOUL

A soul had walked the earthly path, his mission he fulfilled,
And dropped the earthly coil and left it at his will;
Among the souls beyond the veil, he found himself there numbered,
For he had not experienced death. He passed but through a slumber
And as he wakened, quick to see, he found his mission he had not
    filled.
He sought among the teachers old and said, "What is the perfect
    will?"
An ancient sage then to him replied,
"What choice was yours, while in the flesh you did abide?
Was it to serve in fullness there, the God you left to go to earth?
Did you spread love? Did you reach forth, your fellowman to lift?
How come you thought your mission filled, your body then you left?
You shall return again to claim another earthly shell,
And there among man of earth, once again to dwell.
Your work not done has just begun; fear not to then return,
For you have wisdom gathered, son, and much of man have learned
Go forth and seek another shell
And there in love you shall dwell
And tell the tidings of Great Joy . . . of God . . . of Love,
And thus employ all righteousness, and not ill will.
And should your body temple reveal to man of earth a frailty
    perchance,
It is but for the reason, son, desire has so ordained to be,
And not of God but YOUR decree.
Go forth in power and seek to find the selfless ones; the lame, the
    blind;
The lame who faltered along Life's road,
The blind who would not see,
The deaf who would not hear the story told.
Move gently, son, with humble heart, slow of step, falter not!
Reach forth your hand and should man fail to grasp it as you stretch
    it forth
Then let it fall with gentle will

At your side; but press on still.

Press on O son of God, and falter not for man shall learn, man
  shall see

And you O son of God, because of your return to earth,

Shall teach your fellowman that birth

Is not of Soul; it is but flesh—

The Soul moves on in endless quest

Until at last when Light has come because of you, God's eternal son,

Man shall have removed his every blot. Then you can say

'My work is done!' You shall but say your work is done,

But never shall it be my son!

For as you come to us to dwell, you shall continue on.

For you as we, shall find a soul who walks the earthly way,

Whose will it is to speak of God. And you shall go his way.

You shall touch his eyes. He shall see the Light!

You shall speak as in his ear, and he shall hear

As you shall speak. For you shall say, 'No fear, O man of earth, no
  fear!"

God is your counsel. Be bold!

Go forth and speak of Love!

I too, I too have thus so told.

Think not O son of God, your work be ever done,

For man of earth needs Light and Truth

And God needs noble sons.

No more an earthly temple to wear,

No more the physical sorrow bear,

But you shall toil with man of earth—

YOUR WORK IS NEVER DONE."

Peace be with you dear ones! Peace. And as we have previously
mentioned, there are those who are in constant attendance with you,
ever seeking to fulfill their mission. Their work is never done. You
shall tread life's path cautiously. What mean I in so speaking? Not
with fear, but never expect to be fully understood by mortal man
who walks in darkness because of his rebellion unto God.

It is the one who walks in darkness who needs you. It is the one
who because of disobedience, wears a broken body, who needs you. It

is the one who would be hungry who would thirst, the one who has lost his way along the path, who needs you. The physician comes but to he who is ill of body. The teacher comes to the one who is desirous to learn. And never forget, whatever knowledge you possess through your desire to serve God becomes wisdom, and wisdom is priceless.

It is the foolish man who says in his heart, "I have all the wisdom there is. I know." He or she who so states, is the one who shall stumble over their own declaration. We say to you, perfection with few exceptions, has been reached only by a few. The more your knowledge becomes wisdom, the greater your illumination. Dear hearts, you shall always find a place wherein you may share your wisdom. Your wisdom shall never go wanting.

If it were not necessary for you to have wisdom, it would be because God's work on the physical plane has become finished. As long as man continues to make mistakes, as long as man continues his disobedience to God, (and that is the greater mistake), as long as man forgets from whence his all of everything has come . . . man needs guidance. You have encountered many so afflicted.

Do not become dismayed, for when you tenanted your previous physical habiliment you left it by the wayside, because you felt your work was finished. Why did you feel your work was finished? Because you felt self-sufficient. But as you returned to be numbered among . . . and I say returned from the place from whence you came . . . to become numbered with the Celestial Hosts, you found that you had left unfinished business.

The sage of old said to you, "Son, daughter, go find another earthly shell. See yonder! There is a man and woman. They are now preparing a physical vehicle for you. Go and claim it! Your spiritual Mother and your spiritual Father so bid you do. And as you claim the body they are preparing for you, you shall learn to call them mother and father, but do not forget your spiritual parentage! For were it not for your spiritual parentage you would not be.

Go back to earth. Move among your fellowmen. Tell them the story of Light, Life, tell them the story of Love, the greatest Power of God . . . Love. Tell them that strife among men never brings conquest. Tell them the story of Love, and in love there is no selfish conquest. Tell them son and daughter. Return to earth and tell them for their physical time is wasting. It wastes because they are wasting it. Knock upon the door of their hearts while there is yet time for them to hear, lest they too *leave an unfinished pattern.*

Here you are numbered among your fellowmen. You have always been with them. You do not recognize them? It is not strange. Why do you not recognize them? For the reason that when you moved with them before, they were clothed in another habiliment. Do not be confused . . . man of earth endures no trial but what he has earned. Man meets no man of earth, but whom he has met before, and whom he SHALL meet again and again and again, until his portion of life's pattern is finished.

Do not worry. Do not fret, dear hearts. You shall find a place to rest your cross. And it shall not be on an ignominious hill of Golgotha. You shall place it in the fullness of God's eternal Light. Where is your cross? Where do you carry it? What is its shape and likeness? It is but your physical body. That is your cross.

Behold your shadow, or shall I make it definite for you? The shadow of your earthly temple. Stretch forth your arms and what do you find? The shadow of the cross. God's light casts no shadow. God's Light swallows up the shadow, dear hearts. HOW? In this wise, God's Light dispels all physical chaos, all physical strife. God's Light cleanses and purifies man's thinking and there is no shadow in God's Light.

As you stretch your physical hands forth and see the shadow of the cross formed by your outstretched arms, your physical body, you shall say, "O cross of flesh, you no longer crucify me! I AM the resurrection and the life. I AM God's child. You deceive me no more, O physical cross. I no longer hang upon you. I am FREE. You, O physical cross, are now subservient to me! And ere long you too shall be dissolved. Unto the elements from whence you came, I have arisen! Truly the Father and I are one. I have experienced Gethsemane. I have experienced Life over Death. I LIVE."

Dear hearts, now you speak those words to your physical cross. You are the resurrection! You are the Life! Why do you become disturbed? Why do you become overwrought? Why do you become a part of those who do not understand? You can never help man in his darkness by becoming a part of his limited understanding. How shall you help him? Indeed you are to help him. You help him in greater measure by not becoming a part of his chaos, than by, through sympathy, becoming submissive to it. For mind you well . . . the Master of masters never expressed sympathy . . . compassion . . . love was the watchword of the Galilean. Never sympathy.

Sympathy is but a physical attribute and born out . . . and I am going to be rather frank . . . born out of inquisitiveness of the five physical senses. We leave this Truth with you. Love brings about the perfect analysis of Life. Compassion heals. Every seeming obstacle which gives this appearance to you as you walk along the physical path is but a reflection of past experiences. And as you learn, dear hearts, as you learn through love to lift, you not only lift another, but you lift yourself.

You spiritually can never become confused, now mind you that well! You spiritually can never become debased. You spiritually never know weariness. What becomes weary? What becomes debased? Ah, dear hearts, man's mortal thinking, therein lies confusion!

You are spirit *NOW*, as you have always been, as you shall always be. And the reason that you are wearing the present physical body is because you are here on *unfinished business*. And how are you to remain unencumbered from the chaos created by those who are of lesser understanding than yourself? Well, in this wise!

Let your divine intelligence which is your perfect mind, which is Godmind, spiritualize your intellect. Intellect is but mortal you know and it is the composite of the desire created by the five physical senses. It is that which must become spiritualized. It is that which must become cleansed and purged. When intelligence has immersed, has annointed, has baptized the intellect, then dear hearts . . . then dear hearts, shall come to pass the statement of the Nazarene when he said, "Come, let us reason together." For remember, there is a serpent of wisdom that is the all knowing intelligence of God. And there is a serpent of deception that is born out of the weakness of the intellect.

The serpent of wisdom shall devour the serpent of deception. For it is the serpent of deception that grovels upon its belly in the dust, but not the serpent of wisdom.

We love you, we love you, we love you, dear hearts, with an everlasting undying love and in this hour we have endeavored to leave with you a lesson for your fellowman, wherever you may meet them. Do not be given over unto appearances, for in so doing you shall become swallowed up with emotion. *Emotion is not spiritual,* dear hearts. It savors nothing of the serpent of wisdom.

Come down, dear hearts. Come down from the cross of flesh. Come down. Stand in God's Light where there are no shadows. Listen to truth, not the physical intellect . . . you listen . . . and the serpent of wisdom shall devour the serpent of deception and as you listen, you say, "I will Live." Look not for signs. Look not for symbols. Walk forth and into your physical body breathe the breath of Life with an understanding heart. And none of you become over anxious, for over anxiousness is a frailty of emotion and it causes man to run foremost and headlong, so to speak, causing him to trip over his own feet and fall. It will put him quite often on the limb that he is sawing off.

Continue to speak TRUTH to the physical cross, for remember it is a tree. It shall bud. It shall leaf forth. It shall bloom. How? With STRENGTH. It shall no longer persecute and crucify you. It shall serve you as you so intended it to serve you, as the earthy vehicle which shall carry you among man of earth. Through it you shall serve your God, speaking the message of love.

THERE IS NO DEATH

Greetings: There is no Death.

> "There is part of the sun in the apple,
>   Part of the moon in the rose,
>   Part of the flaming Pleiades
>   In everything that grows.
>
> Out of the vast comes nearness,
>   For the God of Love of which man sings
>   Has put a little bit of His Heaven
>   Into every living thing."

Life holds no mystery. From the very beginning, as man of today understands the beginning, *life has been complete.* There is nothing that man can add to life, but there is much for man to enjoy.

Life offers every happiness, peace of mind, health of body. Man should be enjoying these if he but understood the underlying principle of life. What is it? It is simple. It is but *harmony.* Man shall learn to live in harmony with himself first.

What can man offer to his fellowman other than that which he possesses? What else can man share? *Only that which he possesses.* Man shall learn to live in harmony when he learns the meaning of love.

Each Teacher in his time, unto his own people, in his own language, has taught the one and only principle of harmony . . . LOVE. What shall man gain by being at enmity with himself? Your most recent Teacher has said "Love thy neighbor as thyself." Likewise has He stated, "Inasmuch as ye have granted unto the least of these my brethren, ye have granted unto me."

The eternal Principle of Life says to man, "Unto thee I grant, all power is given unto man in heaven and in earth." Let us understand the statement 'in heaven and in earth.' Where is heaven? It has been referred to by the Psalmist of old as the "Secret place of the Most High."

The Master Mystic whom man has accepted as Jesus the Christ, said, "The Heaven of the Almighty is within you." And He made the statement in this wise, "Know ye not that the Kingdom of God is within you?"

God is always in His Heaven, and the only Heaven man shall ever know anything about is the kingdom of God in consciousness. Let man not live in enmity with his neighbor because of *erroneous teachings*.

We are happy to visit with you. We are not strangers among you. Many of our council * are in attendance with you and it shall ever be so. You are never alone. There is no death. *Man, as his creator, is birthless, ageless, deathless.*

A sage of ancient age said this, "Weep not for me. Let not thy days be days of mourning. There is no death. Look! See! From the horizon's edge comes my ship to bear me home. It has passed this way before. Upon this ship we sailed together to reach these shores. Weep not for me. Let not thy days be days of mourning. Death is but sleep. See, in western sky the living glow of the setting sun? Day shall break and it shall rise again. Man shall wake to see its beauty. How long we have been together! We shall meet again. Listen! In thine inner being thou shalt hear the voice in clarion call say to thee, 'I live! There is no death!' Thou shalt tarry for a while, then thou shalt follow on and in the vastness we shall meet and each shall wait."

Desire shall rend asunder the encasement which thought has created to hold man fast, and upon the rising of the sun, man shall choose a woman and there he shall find nestled in her womb, beneath the heart of love . . . a body . . . and as the Son rises in the heavens high, He shall bring that body forth. Each one in his season, so shalt live.†

---

* Council referred to are the sages and teachers of ancient mystical white brotherhood, though unseen to human eye; they are still active, aiding humanity in spiritual service to the Eternal Cosmos—known to us as God.

† Since all life takes it first step from the First cause, the positive and negative of divine essence, or as some would say the male and female principle of infinite cosmic divine energy. The first step into form is light. This is often referred to in metaphysical allegory as the son or the metaphysical child.

This son or light of divine spirit builds the embryo in the womb of the mother. After completing the physical form with its five physical centers, it then builds the seven spiritual centers in the etheric body. The last or seventh center is in the uppermost part of the brain, the pineal gland. When that is completed the body is brought forth away from the protective covering of the womb within the mother.

Turn not thy days into days of mourning, but as thou wouldst stand at the portal of thy dwelling to greet one who had gone forth, but to return, so greet the messenger of sleep. Struggle not with that which expresses the infinite Love of the infinite God.

What man or woman of earth shall lie their body on the couch of rest and say, "Tomorrow I shall see you, my dear." Shall he fear that sleep which erases all claim to evil? Worry not. *Live in Peace.* Strive not against thy fellow man. Become not enrapt with the *viciousness of error. Hold naught against thy fellowman . . . Love!*

Of he who encounters that which man has learned to call strife, hardship, poverty, pain, sorrow, it is but as the handwriting on the wall, which the great seer Daniel was called to interpret. Accept it as a lesson. Look within thine own heart and ask, "What have I done to have brought this to my dwelling place?"

The Master Teacher of your age has likewise said, "Resist not evil. Moreover, overcome evil with good." Who is the man who shall say, "That is too hard for me to do. I cannot forgive. I cannot give good for evil." Such a one is standing in his own light. Out of all the strife of yesteryear, the Kingdom of God now expresses. How come this to be? How come this experience?

Along the life's path of any man, all has not been evil. Good eventually submerges evil into the eternal abyss of its nothingness.

You are familiar with the parable of the story of "The Prodigal Son." Desire took him from the Father's house. Desire for experience directed his attention in another avenue. Much evil seemingly befell him. But at last the Good of which he had been a part from the beginning, and was never separated from, asserted its birthright in the Father. And you will remember he said, "I shall return to my Father's house for there is plenty there."

Look not upon the seeming mistakes of yesteryear. Discard it. In Truth it has never been a part of you. Be there an unpleasantness among you, become mindful of some of your fellowmen who are now enjoying the blessings which you have created, from the heart of love. Remember . . . Never forget! When you have spoken a kindly word, when you have clasped a hand with the warmth of spiritual friendship, and in so doing, have lifted the load from a weary, troubled heart and, perchance, have never again made physical contact with that individual will you from this moment forth, rest in the assurance and the blessed infinite insurance that somewhere along life's path you have dried a tear. You have soothed an aching heart. You have stilled a throbbing breast, wrapt in the throes of anguish.

Rejoice and be exceeding glad for having been an instrument through which God has been able to express! In humility remember, and soon, I assure you, soon that which may appear to be of a problem to you this very moment, shall melt as the ice of your earth place melts in the presence of the vibratory action of the sun's rays. Forget whatever unpleasantness has crossed your path! Call it not back to memory. Let it bury itself in its own dust of its own nothingness.

Likewise, as the Master of Masters said, "If thou be smitten upon one cheek, turn the other." *Love knows no pain! Love knows no sorrow! Love knows no regrets! Regret not one experience through which you have passed.* For each experience along life's path is a lesson, and each lesson well learned is "putting new wine into new bottles."

It is no disgrace for man of earth to become drunken upon the wine of life. Remember! Never forget! Man cannot sprinkle the perfume of kindness on another without a few drops falling upon *himself.*

We welcome you! Your work has just begun. We are aware there is an interest among you because of that which man of earth has learned to call a troublesome season. Be not overly wrought, neither concerned with that which man has learned to call adversity. Each one of you here present shall wake to the morning, when that which gives the appearance of a problem shall have vanished into the nothingness of the night. And the sun of the new day shall swallow it up.*

Lay not your heads on pillows of worry! Let us assure you that harmony shall prevail. Love shall make itself known. Misunder-

---

* Here again the sun or light is used. It was later revealed that they were speaking of the understanding of divine wisdom and its application in a new day or a new age that would dissolve many of man's problems and the confusion they present in the political, economic and social order.

standings shall find themselves as the Prodigal Son on the way back to the Father's house.

There are various forms of that which man has learned to call death; death to one's ideals, aspirations, inspirations. Death to that which man has learned to call the future. Remember dear hearts. Never forget it. Man makes many plans. *God's is the Perfect Idea.* You are a reflection of that perfect idea. When you have learned to cease making plans and particularly planning the life, as it were, of· another individual, there shall be no inharmony.

Expect nothing from your fellow man, other than that which you would freely, lovingly give. *Let plans cease to be!* Place yourself, through your thinking in the heart of the Perfect Idea, and if, in due season you shall find that you have become a stranger to the perfect idea it is because of the confusion which you have permitted to permeate your thought process.

What am I trying to tell you? When it appears to be the most difficult to Love, *express Love in as great a measure as you can!* When it appears to be the most difficult for you to talk with your God, talk with your God! *Pray without ceasing!* How shall man pray without ceasing? Shall he separate himself at certain intervals or periods from his daily occupation or daily routine to pray? I dare say not. Let your every thought be in the attitude of prayer. In this wise shall ye speak in thought. "This which I am doing, I do as unto you the Father."

Should there be a seeming misunderstanding, let your thought to the one from whom the appearance of misunderstanding seems to come, be in this wise. "Dear heart, we are one. *There is no separation in Eternal Principle. There is no division in God. We* have been one from the beginning. We are one now and shall so ever be." You will say to me, "Perhaps." And your questioning shall be within reason. Should you say to me, "Perchance, the one who I am holding in the Allness or the Oneness, perhaps they decide that it shall be different." I repeat . . . Never forget this! *There is no separation spiritually. It cannot be. Love knows no separation.*

Listen! Time is not! Distance cannot be! Memory holds its cherished reflections. Love is eternal destiny.

I trust we have brought you a small portion of leaven with which

to leaven your loaf of life. May you continue to enjoy the beauty and
the love of God as you, through your understanding and the render-
ing of service unto your God, have brought you a goodly portion into
manifestation.

Each one of you are traveling on the highway of spiritual success.
Let nothing deceive you. Be not confused and forsake not that which
you have espoused. Remember the words of the author of the book of
Ecclesiastes, when he said, "Remember NOW thy creator in the days
of thy youth, when the evil days come not, nor the time shall be, that
thou shalt say I have no pleasure in them." Let us assure you, dear
hearts, that you are in the youth of your spiritual growth. With all
the knowledge you have acquired, you are yet babes. The road is long
. . . it is bright . . . and be there a sunset of ignorance, you shall
never see it set.

It has been a privilege, a privileged pleasure to have visited with
you. May your loaf be leavened. I leave you with these words. You
have cast your bread upon the waters of life. They are returning to
you. After many days you are finding them . . . Blessed are you of
the Father's House.

"In my Father's House there are many mansions. If it were not so,
I should have told you. I go to prepare a place for you, that where I
am ye may also be. Inasmuch as I go, I shall return again quickly."
. . . Mansions of experience; the Universe the House. In your quest
you are beholding the Christ, for He has returned to you quickly. He
has beheld your star, heard your call and answered your summons.
Your Christ has arisen in the kingdom of heaven in your consciousness, dear hearts.

So mote it be. Bless you. Bless you.

THE AURIC VEHICLE AND ASTRAL SHELL

Greetings:

All is well! From within the heart of the Eternal Cosmos, we bring a benediction of love and we accept the great love you so graciously share with your fellowmen and shall it ever be a Divine benediction to your soul's consciousness.

Unto the God of the Universe that which is God's and unto the Caesars that which through their desire is rightfully theirs.

It never becomes necessary for one to speak in condemnation toward another who has violated the immutable law of nature, for he himself has pronounced his own judgment. It becomes not necessary in the least wise for man to become concerned with the undoing of another. For he who is of the household of Caesar cannot be turned from his path of destiny, as he so chooses to follow, until his own undoing proves to him that he follows after phantoms of the night, as it were.

And unto he who has cast his lot with the Divine source of all goodness, man can add to him no greater blessing than that which he invokes upon himself by his goodness and kindness.

To know the riches of Heaven is to be at Peace with God, and to be at Peace with God, is to behold naught but goodness in all creation. Man is the noblest handiwork of God and regardless of the path he may choose to follow, that path which leads to the lowest degree of degradation, behold in him the goodness of God, which he in his choice has refused to behold. Such is the law of righteousness.

To those of us who are disembodied, there is no evil. For in your Book of books, it is written, "God's eyes are too pure to behold iniquity."

We are happy to recognize you and accept you as willing channels through which to pour forth the nectar of life. You will find that the yoke of righteousness never becomes burdensome and the path never becomes rough nor dark. There are no chill valleys through which to pass and no insurmountable heights.

This you have already experienced in the path you have so chosen to follow. There is no penalty imposed upon man by God. *God is*

23

just. Man's love for his fellow man is proof sufficient. Man's dislike for man, which man has learned to call hatred is sufficient unto the keeping of the day, but that is the only judgment man shall ever know.

Love begats love. Hatred begats hatred. The magnet of Love attracts the spiritual riches of the Father's Kingdom. Hatred and contempt become a repelling force.

When man shall come to understand that he rules his kingdom, as he so chooses to do, he shall no longer call life a problem. There is nothing problematic about life, other than man so creates it to be. Man should have long since accepted this as truth, had it not been for the fact that *he has been erroneously taught.*

There is but one path. We prefer to call it the path of Fair Play. That is rather a commonplace term, but it is our preference. Set not in judgment of another. May I repeat please? Set not in judgment of another. Let man live freely, to give freely, to accept freely, is but another link in the golden chain of eternity. Wait not for the coming of eternity after you have left your physical coil. Be ever mindful, dear hearts, that eternity has been from the beginning, for the beginning is eternal.

There are certain individuals here upon your mundane sphere of life who labor under the untruth that much of their misbehavior is due to the fact of mischievous, impish, disembodied entities and that is untrue. It cannot be. It is contrary to the law of life. Come! Let us reason together! As man so chooses to live the pattern of life allotted to him in each physical experience, so he builds about him that which we desire to call an astral shell.

May I pause for a moment and give expression to this next thought? What happens when you lay your body upon its couch of rest? Where are you? What takes place?

The Apostle Paul put it in this wise, "There is a natural body and there is a spiritual body." And may I add, man creates this astral body or shell as it were. How? *By every act, thought, word and deed.* Have you ever had the experience of watching a chick pick its way forth from the shell? Quite often it becomes necessary to aid the tiny creature. Why? Because of an over-abundance of calcium in the shell. It makes it rather difficult for the baby chick to gain its release.

What does man do? Every unkind thought, expressed in every unkind word, the result of which becomes an unkind deed, builds, as it were, an over abundance, may I use that term please . . . of calcium in his astral body. Who releases man from this astral shell? No one but man himself. Now, what happens when you lay your body on its couch to rest? You move into this astral shell. It is the means of conveyance, as it were, which carries you to the astral plane of life. But where are you? You are in the Spiritual body which the Apostle Paul referred to. That which the sensitive or psychic or mediumistic individual sees is not the Spirit. It is but the spiritual body which takes on or bears the semblance of Spirit. Now then, if it were possible for disembodied entities to torture, tempt or torment man of earth, to cause man of earth to act unbecomingly, how could this be brought about, if it were possible? But it is not. Would there not have to be some manner of attraction in the mental process of the individual who was enduring the torment, the tempting, as is accredited to the disobedient, disincarnate entity?

Let us reason further, please! Why would those on our side of life be interested in choosing willing, agreeable, susceptible channels, such as you dear people, to voice the message of love, life, and immortality, and become unmindful of mischievous, destructive entities here around about us? This is not conducive to common sense logic, is it?

My next statement is not in the least wise in derogatory mention to the numerous teachers who have written books, upon books, upon books, on that which man has learned to call obsession. May I ask you this question? *When does spirit become spirit?* Only after it has left its flesh habiliment? Reason tells us . . . *NO.* Is that right? Spirit has been spirit from that which man has learned to call the beginning. Is that correct?

Now then, may we reason a little further. What difference is there between you who listen to me and me, who tenants temporarily, this physical body? You are spirit now, are you not? Is that not true?

Student: "Yes."

Do you become spirit to any greater or lesser degree after you are released from the physical body?

Student: "No, but you are oriented differently."

Very well spoken, my good brother. Why then does not man become equally as oriented while in the flesh? Now we are becoming better acquainted with that which man has learned to call "Precepts of Truth." I will grant you freely and wholeheartedly that there is an obsession and it comes about in this wise: Man directs his attention toward obsession from those who are released from the mortal coil and becomes wholly unmindful of the *true* source or center of obsession, which comes from those who are yet in the flesh embodiment. That is your source or seat of obsession.

Student: "You mean a living person could obsess another living person?"

Without any question whatsoever, my friend.

Student: "So long as they are both functioning on the same level of consciousness."

Again wisdom expresses itself. But when in consciousness, man has arisen as it were, above the sordid mundane attraction, he is no longer susceptible to the thought process of those in the flesh, who are bent, as it were, in the direction of causing discomfort. How does this discomfort come about?

You are all acquainted with the Auric Vehicle, are you not? When you come in contact with one who is radiating Love, Peace, Harmony, what is your feeling? It is kindred, is it not? And quite often you say or express yourself in this wise, "I cannot wait until I meet them again." How is this brought about? By the blending of the aura. When there is yet a fragment of distrust, when the old vehicle, as it were, is not thoroughly cleansed, there is a possibility, or may I say, a likelihood of attracting that which is projected through the aura of one who is of the baser nature. Is this understandable?

Student: "I am not a saint. I have made a lot of mistakes."

O, let us reason with you brother. Do I hear you say you have made a lot of mistakes?

Student: "We all have our weaknesses. How do we know?"

Yes, that is true. We grant that. But your greater desire is for the greater spiritual manifestaion, is it not?

Student: "I made mistakes in the past. I don't want to make many more."

Let us not speak of the past, and I do not make that utterance in the measure of chastising. God forbid! Now since you have mentioned it, let us again reason about the past. Never look backward my dear friends . . . never . . . regardless of what the experience may have been. Never look backward. Never become Lot's wife. Never even have the slightest desire to look backward. Never over the shoulder, remember, not even a tiny peek, if I might use that expression, . . . Forward . . . Onward . . . is always Upward. It cannot be otherwise. May I repeat that statement, Forward, Onward, is ever upward.

Student: "May I ask another question?"

Yes, indeed.

Student: "We have reason to believe that at times, in our sleep, we are attending a school, as it were. But we are unable to bring back a clear concept of our experiences. Now what can we do to perfect this memory concept in our consciousness so that we are fully aware of it and are able to bring it back with us? What is the next step?"

May I endeavor to help you. You are justified in acknowledging the fact that you do attend a school, in what you term the sleep state. Your desire is to remember what takes place during that period. Is that what I am to understand?

Student: "To bring back the memory, yes, etch it in our objective brain and consciousness, so that it can help us here and now."

Yes, my dear friend and brother. Yes. There is only one thing for you to do. First, in this wise, give thanks for the realization you have that you are attending school, as you call it, and you have well termed it; then continue with the desire to remember. Let your desire be expressed in gentleness however, not in a commanding or mandatory manner. Before entering the sleep state let that desire be pre-eminent in your very last waking thoughts. Let it not be that I must remember, that I have to remember. Moreover, dear hearts, let it be in this wise, *I shall remember*. It is my desire to remember, that I may share these blessed experiences with those who are less fortunate than myself. If the desire is not answered immediately do not become discouraged. Unto the present hour your discouragements have been few, so proceed on the path which lies immediately before you. May I assure you that with your desire, earnestly and lovingly expressed, you shall bring back into conscious activity all of your experiences.

At first they shall evidence themselves as new ideas. Perhaps you shall wonder how come this idea. Accept it as a memory picture of that which took place while you were in the school of the infinite cosmos. I may leave this thought with you, please. Much of that which you have shared, beyond that which you have gleaned from books, has been the reflection of experiences you have had while dislodged from the mortal coil. It does not all happen in that which you call the sleep state. They are actual living experiences. You may sit in this chair or any other chair and during the period of prayerful meditation . . . and may I use this expression please . . . soar into the vastness of the Eternal Universe and there meet kindred souls and return to your physical body with a complete picture of all which has taken place.

Student: "May I ask another question? One of our group, several times during the last week, nearly left the body. Can you analyze that situation? What is the next step? Can you analyze that and tell her what to do?"

I am to understand from your question that during this period of silence, mental quiescence, or meditation . . . call it what you will . . . you felt as though you were leaving your physical body?

Student: "I felt very light. I felt I was about to float and everything appeared different."

Splendid.

Student: "Everything seemed opaque, nothing was solid."

Beautiful.

Student: "Nothing appeared solid. I was a little frightened and I wondered whether it was advisable to proceed."

My dear friend, would you become frightened if your beloved helpmate would place his hand in yours and say, "Come dear I have something to show you in the adjoining room?" You would have no fear would you?

Student: "No, I would hurry to meet it. I would welcome it."

Yes, will you do something please?

Student: "Yes, certainly."

From this very moment my dear one, annihilate from your thinking every last fragment of fear . . . Remember . . . !

Student: "Fear of anything or anybody?"

Fear of anything that is. No evil can come nigh your dwelling and I am speaking of your physical body. I am speaking of the astral body you are building with the precious thoughts you send forth.

Student: "Why is it that the still small voice that used to instruct me so very audibly, why hasn't that been with me more frequently of late?"

I do not mean to speak to you in terms of reprimand, please understand me.

Student: "I do. I do."

The very thought of fear has closed the avenue through which . . . the still small angelic voice spoke, as you termed it.

Student: "Can I undo that which I did in my stupidity? Can I undo it?"

Look, let us not call it stupidity, my dear one. Let us rather say misunderstanding, shall we? Blessed are you. Can you undo it? Yes, you have already undone, by expressing your willingness to do. We are not here to ill advise you. We have been attracted to this home through what you on the mundane sphere of life call a strange manner. Yet it is not strange. May I say, it is rather in and around the mulberry bush manner. We have visited with you quite often, not only here in this home, but in previous places of abode. We have been with you, dear ones, for what you would term a long time. Now back to your question.

Please do not fear. When you have this experience, learn to say this, "I AM IN PERFECT ACCORD WITH THE PERFECT IDEA, OF THE PERFECT UNIVERSE, WITH THE PERFECT UNIVERSAL SOUL." Remember, dear hearts . . . your soul is a reflection of the Great Oversoul of the Universe and in your quest for Spiritual Truth, Spiritual growth, your soul has become enlarged, as it were, in the fullness of the Great Oversoul of the Universe. When again you have this experience, express a willingness to join the innumerable hosts. I assure you nothing of evil shall befall you.

Student: "Thank you. How can we, how can all of us best serve the White Brotherhood Council. In what capacity are we best fitted to serve?"

My dear ones, as you have served in the past and as it is your desire to serve now, in that which you have learned to call the future, expressing love as you have expressed it.

Be of very great courage. May I say it in this wise, my dear ones, be of a stout heart and in your soul's consciousness at this very moment, let these words fall from the lips of the inner voice, "I LET GO AND I LET GOD. I surrender, fully surrender, in Love and wherever there has been a moment of discord, I grant peace in abundant measure."

Goodnight dear hearts. Bless you! Bless you!

TRUE COMMUNION AND PURIFICATION

Peace, Power and Abundance ever remain your goodly portion. Upon our first visit with you dear ones, we quoted a few lines of verse. May we be privileged to preface our visit at this time with a repetition of those words? They are simple and no doubt you are familiar with them. They are in this wise and give expression to the all inclusiveness of everything that IS.

> "There is part of the sun in the apple,
> Part of the moon in the rose,
> Part of the flaming Pleiades
> In everything that grows.
>
> Out of the vast comes nearness,
> For the God of Love of which man sings
> Has put a little bit of His Heaven
> Into every living thing."

I trust we shall be able to bring you a few morsels from the Great Table of Life, for you will remember the words of the Psalmist of old when he said, "Thou preparest a table before me, in the presence of mine enemies."

Will you visualize this table in consciousness? It is the table within the Holy of Holies upon which rests the Golden Platter wherein is placed the Shew Bread of Life and at either side there stands the Golden Candlestick, in which there is placed the seven candles, lighted, symbolizing the seven planes of spiritual consciousness.

Where shall man find this table, but within the inner sanctum? How long shall man remain satisfied to grope in the darkness of superstition? It is blessed that we find you here assembled, anxious and ready to partake of the Bread of Life in the midst of the glowing flame of purity. Blessed are you among all mankind, for he who pauses during the material turmoil of the day to elevate himself in consciousness, truly he shall not knock in vain, neither shall he seek to receive not.

31

With power the words were spoken, "Knock and the door shall be opened unto you, seek and you shall find, behold I stand at the door and knock."

But . . . this door must be opened from the *inside* and we find the door of your soul's consciousness, not just standing ajar but wide open, ready, eager to admit the living, all abiding presence of the Great I AM consciousness of the Universe. 'I AM' has sent me.

It shall not be too far hence, when the scales of physical blindness shall be removed. May I repeat physical blindness for there is no spiritual blindness. Let that become rooted and grounded in consciousness. What causes that which we refer to as physical blindness? Only that which is perceived by the five physical senses.

Within the inner tabernacle, the secret place of the Most High, the Inner Court, the Holy of Holies, call it what you will, there abides the spiritual Light of God. And it permeates seven vital centers in the spiritual body and thus reflects in the physical body.

How is the superstition and mortal contamination removed from the deceiver or mortal mind, carnal mind? Man for eons of time has been quite satisfied to maintain his residence in the five unregenerated centers. There comes a time however, whatever it may be, when man seeks to know more of his God. Sometimes and quite often it is brought about by some physical chaos and though man has denied the beneficence of prayer, yet shall I say instinctively, intuitively, he resorts to prayer, if it but be three words uttered, "God help me." And those three words, sincerely uttered, are all-sufficient. What takes place?

There is a mountain referred to in the Holy Writ called Mount Zion. Where shall we in consciousness find that mountain? We will find it in the uppermost part of the physical structure. It is quite commonly referred to, in reference to two glands, the pituitary and the pineal gland. Some prefer to say the Pi-neal; we desire to refer in this manner, the pituitary and pineal. *There . . . is the dwelling place of the "GREAT I AM"* the Jehovah, Jahawah of the Universe. How is the ascent made? Through desire, dear hearts.

Do not try to discard one particle of that which you have perceived through the five physical centers. Take it all with you and as you begin the ascent to the pinnacle of Mount Zion, to the dwelling place of the indwelling God, the Power of the Seven Illuminated Centers shall descend and as they do they shall purify that which is unregenerate. "And unto he who followeth me through the regeneration, I shall give unto him the power to reign with me, upon twelve thrones." Man must reign upon the five physical thrones but he must reign upon them with the regenerate power. They shall become sheep in the pasture of the Great Shepherd and no longer wolves of destruction.

Much has been spoken and volumes have been written upon the power of free will. Man is free, free indeed, but there is an unregenerated will. Man is free to taste of that will but when he has come to the bottom of the cup and tasted of its bitter dregs and cries, "Abba Father!" the regenerated Will, which is indeed the FREE WILL or the will of Freedom, shall tear from his eyes the scales, loose from his hands and feet the shackles that bind and in the freeness of the Living God, he shall stand before the table laden with the abundance of spiritual food and there he shall feast and no longer of the forbidden fruit.

Knock beloved, the door shall be opened. Seek! Ye shall find! Ask and it shall be granted unto you, for the Great Oversoul of the Universe shall never place in your hand a serpent instead of a fish and neither shall the Great Oversoul of the Universe place in your hand a stone instead of bread.

Within your consciousness is the well of Living Waters. You have but to drink of it. Truly it shall become the wine of Life unto your Souls. Remember you are the Christ of God incarnate in the flesh. You are the honored guest at the wedding of Cana. Turn the water into wine, dear hearts. Drink of it freely, for it shall cause the marrow of your bones to become rich, and the fiber of your body to become strong.

Fear not to ask of the Great Creative Power man has learned to call God. If you ask in small measure, in a small measure you shall receive. Ask in abundance and abundance you shall receive.

Remember, dear hearts, *Never Forget* these, my parting words. Share when you can, in the measure in which you have been prospered to share, if it is but a kindly smile, the warmth of your hand in the hand of another. Your hand placed in the benediction of Love upon a weary brow. Share, dear hearts, for as you share, your coffers shall become filled, your granaries shall become filled to overflowing and the window of your heaven, the doors of your heaven shall open wide and shower upon you innumerable blessings.

This law is in your keeping. Use it wisely. Do not measure yourself short with the yardstick of judgment by measuring the frailties of your fellowman.

We thank you for this opportunity. Bless you. Bless you.

Peace, Peace, Peace. So mote it be.

HAVE NO FEAR—GOD IS YOUR BANKER

Greetings:

"Thou in whose image and likeness we are created, in Spirit, and in Truth. Thou whom down through the ages we have learned to call God. We give thanks for thine innumerable blessings, and before the altar of righteousness, we would lay our gift and go forth and make peace, but to return before the altar and offer our gift.

"We thank thee, Father, for thy greatest gift of all, the gift of Eternal Life. We thank thee that in this great plan, there is no death, that at the proper moment and the proper conditions, we can hold communion with those of our loved ones who have preceded us through the change called death, which is but a transition.

"Thou art a gracious God. Somehow, Father, from the innermost depths of our being, we do not ask of thee, we come not with pleading, we rejoice . . . we give thanks! Thou are a kindly God. We have beheld the Star in the East and may we never remove our sight from the brilliance of thy love.

"And, as we approach the season of the year that man has set aside for the adoration unto the infant Jesus, may we behold the true significance, the birth of the Christ within.

"Father, may we know nothing other than to share thy love. As best we know how, Infinite Heart, we surrender our body, soul, and spirit to Thee. Use it. Somehow, may it become of greater service than in that which we have learned to call the past.

"Through thy infinite law of love, we shall return to the altar after having made peace with thy children, and with our fellowman. Accept our humble offering. Omain."

Fear not, O man of earth! Love is the guiding light. Cast not thy gaze toward thy feet, for within behold the light. No stumbling blocks along your path, no pitfalls you shall find. Put thy hand in the hand of God! He will lead thee. Free, thy step shall be. Unfettered thou shalt walk. No power, how great or small it be, shall injure thee in thy walk along life's road. One step at a time, with even stride, with thy hand in the hand of Love.

35

What shall we share with you this evening? What is your desire? We are at your bidding.

Student: "How should we proceed to share these lessons? Have you any suggestions?"

I am very happy that you placed it in the manner in which you have, "Have we any suggestions?" We never advise; we never command; neither do we make demands. It is ever but a suggestion. My dear one, our suggestion is in this manner . . . there is, as we have given to you in a previous lesson, but *one idea. That is the supreme idea, the perfect idea, the God idea.*

Whatever your desire . . . the sincere desire of your heart's consciousness may be . . . you shall recognize after you have given this thought spiritual deliberation. We suggest that you hold it in the uppermost chamber, as it were, in consciousness. Bathe it with love, and when it shall have become a part of the divine idea, it shall be revealed to you.

You now have a desire of what you would like to do. It is not in error. However, do not act in haste. The perfect plan of man bears fruit when it becomes co-relative with the Divine Idea. It has ascended from the depths of mortal conception, through the light of Spiritual Love, and arises and makes contact with the perfect idea. Thus man experiences that which he has learned to call success.

Many a well laid plan has become dashed to pieces upon the rocks of despair for the reason that it never reached the sanctum of the Divine Idea. All success that man has ever known or shall know, is that plan which has had its birth in the womb of Divine Idea.

While I am speaking to you, I am mindful of certain ones here in this group who are slightly confused, due to the fact that recently several doors have been closed and seemingly prevented them from that, which in mortal consciousness, spelled progress to them at the time. It is unnecessary for me to single you one from the other. You know to whom I speak. Be not discouraged, children of the Father's house, be not discouraged, *for never has a door closed, but what it shall open again, and beyond that door there shall be open portals to which you shall find no doors. Never acknowledge defeat.*

It has been so said that opportunity knocks at man's door but once. That is untrue. It only becomes true to the degree that man may hear it but once, for the reason that he becomes confused. *Opportunity knocks with every breath you breathe. God is not a God of limitation, but as we have previously stated ageless . . . birthless . . . deathless. You are children of the living God. What then is your inheritance? Is it less than the father's? It cannot be.*

May I leave the passing word with you? *Before you ask, decide what you are going to do with that which is granted to you, after you have asked.* Let your prayer be not in a beggarly or niggardly manner. Let it be a selfless prayer. Erase the small 's' from the word 'self,' and in its stead place the large 'S' or the capital 'S' as you would term it: the divine Self, the oneness with the great oversoul.

YOUR GOD IS AN ETERNAL BANKER. Resources of the universal are at his command. It needs must be. He is the creator, and to your credit, as a child of God, there are many negotiable drafts written; you are now in consciousness, in possession of every spiritual draft the Father has written. *They are written in your name to your credit. Acceptance . . . receiving . . . appropriating . . .* it is that simple.

There is nothing complicated in your relationship to God. Man has complicated matters, if I may use those terms. Man creates his own problem. Will you place your signature upon the drafts you now possess and go to the father's bank and pass them, as it were, to the paying teller and receive your abundance.

Are you asking me, "how shall I place my signature?" You are justified in asking this question. Here is the answer . . . *full and complete surrender to God.*

But you will say to me, "That is rather lame advice, a lame suggestion, is it not? Are you telling me to become unconcerned with the things of this world?" Ah, no, my dear children, not so! There is a manner in which to become concerned with the things of this world, as you would say, spiritually concerned.

Steeped in the depths of mortal reasoning, man becomes confused. Hear me! Cash your check! Receive your spiritual riches and you shall then be able to cope with that which heretofore has spelled confusion! Have no fear!

Our visit shall be very brief. It is our desire that you continue your visits one with the other. Discuss the happy experience you have had;

talk of the blessings you have experienced, and in the inner depths of your soul's consciousness, nurture that of good. Nurture it silently, that of good, which you desire to share with your fellow man; then it shall become as fertile seed sown in fertile soil and it shall bring forth its own fruit, after its own kind.

Have you ever stood beneath the branches of a stalwart oak tree and, looking up at those branches, beheld a tiny acorn dangling from a tiny twig? What is in the heart of that acorn? The acorn knows only this, "I shall fall to the ground and, undisturbed by man, I shall find myself nestled in the bosom of Mother Earth, and I shall become a mighty oak, and upon my branches shall hang acorns, myriad in number."

Sons and daughters of the Father's House, you are mighty oaks in the father's forest. Your branches of love hold acorns myriad in number. They shall fall. Let them fall silently, lovingly, tenderly. Do not disturb them. Let them find lodgement in an aching heart and they shall spring forth as a mighty oak.

Thank you, goodnight.

MORTAL WILL VERSUS DIVINE WILL

In the bond of Spiritual friendship, we gather with you before life's altar, above which burns the flame of purification. The altar not made with human hands, moreover with precious jewels of love and the flame unfed by human hands.

Since you are not alone but moreover in attendance by some member of our council, your brothers in Spiritual Love, we are mindful of your every summons. We recognize that we are free to talk with you and not particularly in a manner of chiding in the leastwise.

Each thought, whether it is formulated in speech or not, sends forth its particular radiance. As soon as man of earth thinks, his thought becomes an illumination and it disturbs the ethers, thus creating a summons. The author of the book of Ecclesiastes, in your present Holy Writ, and I say in your present Holy Writ . . . gives man, among the many statements, this statement; "In the making of many books is there a great folly. Therefore the Teacher sets into being acceptable words." It is wise for man to gain knowledge. Solomon, whom man has called the wisest man, was wise, but not the wisest man. Godman is the man of all wisdom. Godman is the unwritten book, the Akasic record of life.

We have no quarrel with man's desire to glean knowledge. Solomon said, "Get wisdom, get understanding. Wisdom is the principal thing, and with all thy getting get understanding." As you of the earth plane express yourself relative to time, sometime in what you have learned to call the past, in this present itinerary of life, you made this statement: "I wish we could find some manner in which to clarify all that which seems rather misunderstandable to us." Is that correct?

Student: "That is right."

During our first visits with you . . . and may I refer to them please? We made this statement . . . Always remember it . . . We impose no hardship, we make no demands, and neither do we command. You are desirous of understanding the potency of will?

There is but ONE Will and that is the Will of God. Some man of

39

earth has coined this statement, "The longest way round is the shortest way home." That is merely a figure of speech but the direct route to the Father's House is the shortest way. In previous lessons much has been said of Love and you shall continue to hear of it. That is the first step upon the path which leads to the Perfect Will.

You have read of the life of Guatama Buddha? Have you come across this experience in his life? In the life's journey of Buddha he was confronted by one who was antagonistic to his teaching. The individual vilified him, upbraided him and Buddha, Guatama Buddha stood in reverent silence.

Let us consider love and silence as handmaidens along life's path. Because of the continued silence of Buddha his accuser became caustic in his accusations and finally, when he had exhausted all his mental bombast, Buddha replied in this manner, "My brother have you finished?" His accuser replied in this manner, "I have finished, but I am not your brother."

Love expressed itself. Buddha's reply was in this manner, "We are brothers, you are my brother." Listen, carefully listen, this will answer something for you . . . To his accuser Buddha said, "If you were to offer a gift and it were not accepted, whom would remain the recipient of the gift?" and after some mental contemplation his accuser answered and said, "The giver or the extender of the gift."

Buddha replied in this manner, "My brother you have well spoken and all that of vilification you have offered me, in love I refuse to accept. Therefore, you the creator of this gift, are the recipient and it remains with you and only through love can you return it to its source of Nothingness."

Listen dear ones, why have I asked you to listen patiently? May I answer it for you? Along life's path . . . not that we were disagreeably inharmonious . . . and when I say along life's path I am referring to previous incarnations, you as all others, who have crossed life's sands, were young in your soul growth. There were mistakes which man has placed in the category of error. Error perhaps is the better manner in which it be expressed.

Now, let me return momentarialy please to the words of the Galilean when He said, "Forgive us our debtors . . ." not transgressors . . . "Our debtors, as we have in equal measure forgiven our debtors." That is the original statement in the Aramaic. Through translation crowded with erroneous thinking on the part of mortal mind, it has been prostituted to read, as embodied in your present Writ, "Forgive us our debts as we forgive our debtors."

The humble Galilean went on in his elucidation to make this statement, "For if man forgiveth not his debtors, God cannot forgive his debts." Men of earth who have branded themselves atheists . . . *and there are no atheists* . . . man may become antagonistic, but in the true sense he never becomes an atheist. Impossible.

The breath of life he breathes, the blood as it pulsates through his body, that which he accomplishes is in his consciousness . . . a mute recognition of the Life Principle of God. But the atheist says this, "Your God is unjust. He will not forgive you if you do not forgive." Let us analyze the statement. How is forgiveness brought into being? Man must give the new for the old. Where does man find the new? In the heart of love.

May I make this analogy please? If in this room you desired to place new furnishings and you placed them here in the midst of the furnishings, which are now in this room, they would not harmonize perhaps, would they? Your room would become overcrowded. What would be your first procedure, dear hearts? To remove the present furnishings, is that right? Now we are approaching the avenue of reason.

Give the new for the old. Man must make a complete eradication of the old, that God may have complete possession. If man holds on to old grudges, how can God become supreme ruler? Does it make sense? And if the original Scripture were brought down to present day man, *uncontaminated by erroneous translation,* to suit the mental whims of the translators, man would know the Truth of his oneness with his God.

Why am I relating this to you, dear ones? We heard you make this statement that you "Demanded of God." You did not demand. What did you do? Forcibly you cleaned the chamber of all clutter of the past, all the accumulation that gave evidence in the physical body of distress, you removed. You did not demand of God.

Student: "Was I wrong?"

Indeed not, I prefaced my statement did I not? We were in

agreement with you. What did you do? You spoke of it as a demand, but dear one you became in absolute agreement with God. You accepted, in its fullest measure the perfect idea. You made no plans, did you?

Student: "No."

Did you say I shall do this or I shall do that? . . . I shall do this or I shall do that? No indeed, you are not caustic in your statement, you are not vicious. Let us consider another statement of the humble Galilean. He said . . . listen carefully . . . "Agree with thine adversary, agree quickly with thine adversary, while thou art in the way with him, lest the adversary deliver thee to the officer and the officer deliver thee unto the prison chamber and thou shalt not come forth therefrom, until thou hast paid the last farthing."

Now I have purposely made an omission, that I may repeat the statement, here is the statement in its full content, "Agree quickly with thine adversary while thou are yet in the way with him, lest the adversary deliver thee unto the officer (possession) and the officer deliver thee unto the judge (false recognition, false accusation) and the judge deliver thee or cast thee into the prison." . . . prison? . . . continued recognition of mortal torment . . . "and thou shalt not come forth therefrom, until thou hast paid the last farthing."

You agreed with the adversary. Quickly you beheld the adverse circumstance and you passed no evil judgment, hence your release from the prison chamber quickly. Let us consider the word agreement. It is not as man of the present day interprets the word agreement. The humble Galilean meant but this in using the word agreement . . . Behold the error, become cognizant of, recognize that of error and release it and *in doing so accept freedom.* May I in graciousness ask one favor of you?

Student: "Yes, indeed."

Will you erase the word demand and in its place recognize the word agreement? You made no demand of God, for it is not necessary to make a demand of God. If there were any demand made, you demanded Satan to be gone!

Student: "I understand."

The satanic force of accumulated error and satan said, "I will clear this chamber," and God entered and the debt was redeemed. Let us go back to the statement of the Nazarene when he said, "Thy will be done in earth as it is in Heaven."

Our good sister in what she has called a demand made that statement in a most emphatic manner. She said, "Get thee hence O thou evil!" Therefore you cleansed the flesh and whatever man of earth did for your body was in accord with Divine Idea, the perfect will of God. All of love which you had shared along the path of life, all the silence which you had maintained in the face of every adversity, as Buddha stood in silence before his accuser, placed their hands together. Love and silence said, "We are one." They preceded you on the path to the Father's House.

Man uses a will which is mortal will. It is unregenerated will. It is a falsifier. It is a liar, as Paul termed it. And when it is eradicated from consciousness through Love . . . through Tolerance . . . through the silent avenue of prayerful meditation, the Perfect Will, may I say, expands in consciousness and in due season, envelops the entire consciousness of man. And the mortal will is lost in its own eternal abyss of nothingness.

Student: "Do you mean that in a sense, if we command error to leave through that command, as error moves out Divine Will moves in?"

Yes, my brother. God is desirous of moving in. God's Will is the Perfect will. God is desirous of ruling that which he created.

Student: "What we have to do is to clean the house of our mind?"

YES, man limits God. God is not demanding. God is not forceful. God is all Tolerance, all Patience and when man becomes patient as unto God, when man becomes tolerant as unto God . . . how does he accomplish this? Through Love, dear hearts, love is the first step, there is no other procedure. Listen to me, has it not so proven to be in your life?

When adversity confronts you, with Love make this statement, "You do not exist, you are no part of God, God has not created you, you came out of the reservoir of eternal confusion. I will have no part of you. I am patient with God. God is patient with me." You understand, dear heart?

After man has emptied the inner chamber of all clutter, he fills the emptiness with Love. It is as simple as that. It does not become necessary for man in the physical to extend his hand and say, "Please forgive me if I have wronged you." Your paths may never cross physically, but with every breath you breathe, with every thought you think, with every pulsation of blood through your body, your paths *spiritually continue to cross.* Thus in sacred reverence, place your gift before the altar of life, where upon this visit, we greeted you . . . and in thought meet your brother.

Would you feel in the leastwise indebted, in this manner greet him, "All is forgiven, there is no malice, no contempt. We are one." Then lift your gift upon the altar beneath the flame of purification and in humble genuflection accept the full measure of God's forgiving, healing, prospering, sustaining Love.

Student: "Thank you, we need this guidance, Thank you."

If I have helped you, may I take my departure. Before I entered, my dear brother, we recognized your thanks because of your summons to us with grateful supplication. We bid you adieu.

FROM MORTAL CONSCIOUSNESS TO CHRIST CONSCIOUSNESS

There is a way which seemeth right unto a man but the end thereof is death, and in the realm of truth, man comes to understand that there is no death. What shall be done with the statement? Is it false? What is the meaning of death? Is it the extinction of life, the annihilation? I dare say not!

How shall man define the word death, the word die? It is rather simple, not in the leastwise complicated. It is from the ancient Sanskrit meaning "to change."

You will remember the words of the Apostle Paul when he said, "Yea, though I live—I die daily." Those words were well spoken and fortunately, through the various translations from the original Scripture, they have never been changed. To many, those words seem rather contradictory. How could a man live and die daily?

You will remember likewise the words of Job when he said, "If a man die shall he live again?" It sounded as though Job were questioning the possibility of the continuity of Life. No, Job was not questioning. Job said, "How can a man live and ever die?" Job was *positive* that *life was everlasting principle.* To die is to become free from all that which is . . . no longer useful . . . to human kind.

What happens to man when he has a change of thought? He continues to move about among his fellowmen, does he not? What has happened? As the orthodox theologian says, "He has become crucified with Christ." Now let us clarify that statement, if we may. But first let us separate the mixture, as it were.

Christ is power. Christ is the incarnate power of God in form, or in physical manifestation. Jesus was the man and I daresay was a man unregenerate, until, by revelation through elevation in consciousness, he became aware of his Christhood, his sonship, with the Father. It was the physical body of the man Jesus which experienced crucifixion and you will remember, the body left the spirit. The spirit did not leave the body.

Unto what did the Apostle Paul "die daily?" Unto the error of the unregenerated will. How? Through the purification of his thinking.

45

You will remember that the Apostle Paul likewise said . . . and listen carefully, dear hearts, to this statement . . . "Let there therefore be in you, the same mind as was and is in Christ Jesus." Not Jesus Christ . . . Christ the Power . . . Jesus was the mortal man.

You will likewise remember that the humble Galilean said, "Marvel ye therefore not at the things which I do, for even greater things than these shall ye do." Likewise he stated, "And unto he who followeth me through the regeneration, when the son of God shall set upon his throne, I shall give him to reign or to rule over twelve thrones, over the twelve tribes of Israel, over twelve thrones, upon twelve thrones."

He who goes forth, my dear hearts, in *quest of spiritual growth, spiritual beauty, is Israelitish.* He is of the Tribe of Israel. He has progressed from the land of Egypt, from the darkness of the unregenerated will; has passed through the Red Sea of superstition and is moving on to rule upon the thrones in the Holy of Holies, in the inner sanctum with the son of God.

How shall he rule with the son of God? In no other manner than to rule with himself, for is he not the son of God? Does man incarnate in the flesh become the child of God, the son of God, because he ascribes himself to some Ecclesiastical rule? I dare say not. How is this brought about, dear hearts? Only in one manner, *through the regeneration—through the regeneration of the mortal will, into the perfect will of the only God of the universe, the living God.*

What is the first procedure? First we shall give recognition to the fact that there is but *one mind* and *that is the mind of God. Man has no mind. In pure spiritual essence, man is mind.* Man is pure unadulterated substance but he lost his way in the wilderness of Egypt.

You are all acquainted with the parable or the story of the Prodigal Son. It therefore becomes unnecessary for me to relate it to you in detail, but remember this part of the parable. When the son had become tired, as it were, of feeding upon the husks, not even the corn, just the husks, he said, "I shall return to my Father's house, for therein is plenty." And may I call this to your attention? As he returned, the Father saw him coming afar off, for the reason that though the son had diverted his attention from the Father, the Father had never taken his sight, his attention, from the son. Let us consider the remainder of the story in symbology.

The Father called for the servants to bring forth the Scarlet Robe . . . scarlet, symbolic of love. The Robe . . . symbolic of protection. The Father called for sandals and he placed them upon the son's feet, the Feet . . . symbolic of understanding. New sandals, please remember, clothing the understanding with protection, the newness, the fullness of understanding.

Understanding came to the son while he was feeding upon the husks. And the Father placed upon the finger the Golden Ring . . . gold the precious metal . . . the ring, without beginning, without end, symbolizing *the oneness of eternal principle in God.* The Father commanded that the fatted calf be slain and the feast be prepared, symbolizing, dear hearts, the spiritual abundance of the Father.

All of this, dear hearts, all of this and more and more and more belongs to man. It is his. It has been his priceless possession from the beginning. But he has not accepted it. Therefore the unregenerated will shall pass through the crucifixion. It shall pass through the change of death. It shall die but to live!

I leave you with this closing statement. The humble, lowly Galilean in the prayer of prayers, admonished man to pray after a certain manner, and in that prayer, He embodies these words, "And forgive us our debtors as we have forgiven our debtors." And He completed that portion of the prayer by saying, "for if ye forgive not . . . for-if-ye-forgive not." And in the original Aramaic, the remainder of the statement was written in this wise, *"how can your heavenly Father forgive you?"*

What shall we do with the word forgive? We shall understand it to mean *give up the old for the new.* Dear hearts, *all of that in man's affairs can never change until he gives up the old manner of thinking for the new. That is the first step upon the path of regeneration.* It is unfortunate that man has been fearful, fearful indeed to invoke the perfect will of the Father, for the reason that he has been erroneously taught that pain, sickness, poverty, unhappiness, is a punishment of God. That is a blasphemous error, blasphemous to the Almighty.

The perfect will of God is health of body, peace of mind, plenty of everything there is; a comfortable home, an abundance of food, all there is in creation to bring every happiness to man. Man cannot blame his neighbor, neither can he blame God.

Do not be afraid to say, "Thy will be done." Remember to say, "In earth as in heaven," is to declare the regenerating of the five physical centers by the spiritual illumination of the Seven SPIRITUAL CENTERS so commonly referred to as the *seven heavens*.

Yes, let man be agreed with the Apostle Paul as the Apostle Paul sought to free himself of the rebellious heart. One Mind! *One mind,* dear hearts, *the mind of God!* And when man elevates himself in consciousness because of proper, constructive, spiritual, thinking, he is rising *out of mortal intellect into spiritual intelligence*—and returning to the Father's House . . . *divine mind* . . . as the Prodigal Son in the parable we just considered.

Bless you, dear hearts, bless you. Live in your freedom of your birthright in God. You are now children of the living God, joint heirs from the beginning. And I say to you . . . there is no end . . . from the beginning and there is no end. Eternity is now. There is no time. Distance cannot be. Memory holds its cherished reflections. Love is eternal destiny.

Peace, Peace. Thank you.

THE HEALING POWER OF LOVE

We would like to engage a few moments of your time relative to the healing love of God. Jesus of Nazareth well understood the story of creation and when he said, "In earth, as it is in Heaven," he was referring to the manifestation of the indwelling, all abiding, ever present Christ of God. The physical body he referred to as the "earth" for you remember he said, "The kingdom of God is within you." And since God is ever in His Heaven, therefore man must needs understand that HEAVEN IS A STATE OF CONSCIOUSNESS.

You have listened to previous discourses relative to the illuminated centers, the Seven Spiritual Centers and the five physical centers. Together they comprise the twelve thrones. Throughout the physical body there are trillions of minute cells. They are intelligences in their own right. They respond to whatever message is sent to them. God is Spirit. *Spirit is indestructible.* Man is Spirit, *not a Spirit. Man is Spirit.* Not in the image and likeness of God but *the image and likeness of God.* And since God is indestructible, man likewise is indestructible and he should have long since known this to be not true, but TRUTH, had he been properly taught.

Therefore, God is birthless, ageless, deathless. Man, his image and likeness is as God is birthless, ageless, deathless. When man says, "I am this" or "I am that" which is spoken contrary to Truth, he is BLASPHEMING GOD. Man cannot be sick, neither can he experience poverty. Neither can he experience failure. Only as he so declares it to be in his thinking. And that, he continues to do, as long as he remains a part of the unregenerated will.

But when the five physical senses have become purged because of man's desire so to do, man no longer thinks in error, hence he can no longer speak in error. For man to say, "I am sick," is declaring that God is sick and that is error. That is blasphemy. For man to say, "I cannot do it," is saying God cannot do it. Each time man speaks in error, he is divorcing himself from God, but as soon as he recognizes his oneness with the Father, behold ALL things become new, new in consciousness.

Therefore, when the physical body is in a state of ill repair, it is because man, over a period of time, has limited the action, manifestation of the Power of God. Therefore, Jesus of Nazareth was expediently wise when he said, "In earth (in the physical body) as in Heaven" (in Spirit, in consciousness). As soon as man grasps the enormity of the GREAT WHITE LIGHT OF TRUTH, as soon as he learns to say, *"I am all power, I am all abundance, I am all strength, I am all health,"* he is dethroning THAT which he has given abiding place to, by the deception of the five unregenerated physical senses.

Each time man says "I am power," each tiny cell throughout the physical body says, one to the other, "Do you hear the command? We are *power,* let us be up and doing." *Thus the giant of helplessness becomes the giant of power.*

Man has been led to believe that he must deny himself of all that which is good and live in the most, shall I say, impoverished manner, that he may worship God. Why should God have created all things FIRST and man last? But you will remember as the story is narrated in your present Writ, in the book of Genesis, after God had created man he said to man, "What shall we name this? And what shall we name that?" Truly God could have named what he had created, could he not?

But the first expression of free will . . . free will . . . free in the power of God, God gave to man to name and man has been naming ever since. But through erroneous teachings he has learned to name in error, hence he has gradually prostituted the power of Infinite Free Will.

A writer of hymns gave title to one of his hymns in this manner, "My Father is rich in houses and lands. He holds the wealth of the earth in his hands" and well did he speak. Listen, dear hearts. Men and women have chanted, have sung, have repeated those words time over and time again have clapped their hands and stamped their feet and became elated over them and have said, "Truly my Father is rich in houses and lands" but to deny the very substance of which they were singing by saying, "I must be very humble, I must not expect too much of God." That is inconsistent, is it not? Yes, the Father is rich. Truly he owns the cattle on a thousand hills, truly he does, and you are co-heir with the Father. *What belongs to the Father belongs to you.*

Would you like to read the Lord's Prayer in its entirety; the prayer that the humble Galilean prayed WITH the Father? It is unselfish. It is beautiful. You will find it by reading the entire Seventeenth Chapter of St. John.

That is the Lord's Prayer. The pattern of prayer you read in the Sixth Chapter of Matthew, from the ninth to the fifteenth verse, is a pattern of prayer after which Jesus admonished man to pray. If you desire to do a little comparison may I suggest that you correlate that prayer with the Twenty-third Psalm and you will make a discovery. For the Psalmist begins by saying, "The Lord is my Shepherd, I shall not want," and the Galilean said, "Our Father which art in Heaven, hallowed, loving, adorable is thy name." Read them verse by verse and you will find that the Galilean is placing the Twenty-third Psalm in acceptable words to the Great Oversoul of Life, the I AM, ALL PERVADING PRINCIPLE.

When I tenanted a physical body, there was a very dear woman brought to me and all the doctors of her day said, "You do not have long to live. Your heart is wearing out. You had better put all your affairs in order." Somehow at that early day, the voice of Truth welled up within my consciousness and among the first revealings I had, came this statement for her, "My heart is right with God." And, as this statement was revealed to me, it came as each pulsation of the blood. Listen! "My heart . . . is right . . . with God." The heart, the flesh heart is a muscle, dear hearts, and it is involuntary, as every other part of the body, and is under command of God.

Do you have to stop to remember to breathe? I dare say not. Yet your lungs continue to expand and contract and the heart continues to expand and contract. Why? In the brain are cells and when those cells no longer function properly something happens to that particular part of the physical anatomy they control!

Would you enjoy another morsel of good reading? You will find it in the very last chapter of the New Testament, in the Twenty-second Chapter of Revelations and indeed it is a revelation. For, therein you will read about the tree and the river of waters and the tree bearing twelve manner of fruit, in its season. And the twelve branches and the leaves upon the twelve branches given unto the Nation for the healing thereof. And "nations," wherever you find it mentioned in the Scripture, means *"man of earth, humankind."*

In the Scripture you will read of the "Pillars of the Temple of Solomon." Metaphysically we will refer to them as the great ganglia, ganglionic system of nerves, the Pillars of the Temple of Solomon, the "Tree of Life" if you please. And from the uppermost part of That Tree are twelve cranial nerves . . . listen, dear hearts . . . the twelve branches upon which you will find the leaves of healing.

How is man to use God? Is God to be used? . . . Truly so. Used righteously and never abused. Man shall use God by declaring God in Truth. Therefore, may I admonish with you, never hesitate, have no fear to say, "Thy will be done."

MENTAL DIET

In unity of purpose . . . the words were well spoken, "As a man thinketh in his heart, so is he." *ALL power comes from within* and to whatever degree a man thinks, so he orders his conduct, so he attracts to himself those who are necessary to meet, to complete the fabric of life.

As a man thinks, through desire he creates the environment in which he moves. Likewise well spoken were the words, "It is not that which goeth into the mouth which defileth a body, for is it not caught up with the draft and becomes no more? But it is that which proceedeth forth from the mouth which defileth."

As we discussed with you in previous communications, all things in moderation, and in this very sanctum when the hand of fellowship was extended to you from our Council, you were not asked to forsake or discard, only as your reasoning revealed to you.

There are so many groups of people gathered together who place stress and strain upon the care and keeping of the body, because of that which is eaten and that which is taken in the form of liquids. That seems to hold preeminence in their routine of discipline and their thinking is secondary. We suggest that the mental stomach be well taken care of with clean, pure, wholesome, *mental food.*

The physical body is a laboratory in itself, and has been so created that its treatment in moderation will take care of whatever is accepted in the form of foods or liquids. It is likewise written, "Be ye therefore not given over unto gluttony." That statement is not alone relative to physical food. It refers as well to man's thinking.

Man should be as cautious in what he reads and how he thinks, as well as with the food he eats, to sustain the physical body. *Soul growth should be man's first consideration,* and that is through thought. Man only speaks as he thinks. Personalities change. Man creates through his thinking the personality appropriate for every environment in which he finds himself, and that is through thinking.

Likewise you will read the statement, "All power is given unto man in heaven and in earth." In some translations you will read it in this manner, "All power is given unto man, in heaven and ON earth." But when man considers his physical body as the composite of physical elements, he shall understand that he has complete command over those elements by his thinking.

Let us consider the farmer. He prepares his soil by plowing, disking, and harrowing it and placing rows upon rows in which to plant the seed. Certain rows or grooves are deeper than others, depending upon the type of seed to be sown. And so it is with man. As man thinks he plows, disks and harrows the soil of his brain and when he is in earnest, zealous, sincere, the rows he creates are deep. They are not shallow and the seed is therein dropped and carefully nurtured.

Likewise you read the parable of the sower who went forth to sow. Some seed fell on barren soil. Some fell on rocky soil and was burned by the heat of the sun and perished, while other seed was sown IN . . . not on . . . fertile soil. And the seed sown in fertile soil is the seed that produces the full fruition.

SPIRITUALLY, MAN IS A GIANT. SPIRITUALLY, THERE IS NOTHING IMPOSSIBLE FOR MAN TO ACCOMPLISH. God-man never becomes defeated. Therefore, keep the mental soil well tilled and your harvest shall be great. Remember one of the previous lessons, there are trillions upon trillions of minute cells throughout the physical body. They are as stars in what you have learned to call the heavens, and when properly spoken to, shine and twinkle with the brilliance of power and so regenerate the earthly form and that which man calls ill health, sickness, cannot exist. Remember it is not that which goeth into the mouth which defileth the body, it is that which cometh forth.

Woe betide unto the man or woman who suffers with mental indigestion. For it is as the farmer who sows various varieties of seed in the same rows. What would be the crop to come forth? So it is with man's thinking. Find the choice seed and plant it in deep furrows with love. Nurture them with patience and sincerity and there can be no lack, no want, no limitation.

The crooked path shall become straightened and the dark way shall become brightened. The sun of Love shall warm and bring forth in bountiful fruition, the seeds you have sown, the sun . . . the sun of Faith. Truly the statement so written, "Though man's faith be no larger than the mustard seed it shall remove mountains." Man never encounters a mountain greater than doubt. Doubt is a deceiver. It is as the thief in the night. Remove it . . . remove it . . . do not let it come nigh your dwelling. Never doubt. Learn to say and learn to mean it, "I am the all of everything of good."

We have tried to give this lesson as an obligation to all, to the beginner as well as the scholar. I am leaving this one word with you, as you progress in your various duties as they shall be assigned to you, you shall at long last tear the scales from the eyes of the doubter, loose the hands and feet that are bound. Your work has been well laid for you. For the reason that you shall work together in harmony.

Myriad are the ones who have latent talents, but for the reason they have felt underprivileged, they have kept them buried. Many have been denied the beneficence of those talents. So you dear ones shall find a place for each one and as you enable them to express their talents and the fruition of the talents comes into being, each shall share their talents with the other, the abundance thereof. And he who has been considered, himself shall rejoice because he has been able to contribute his portion to the community in which they live and to the world at large. Because at last shall come into manifestation, that which man has spoken of, has written much about and done very little about . . . the UNIVERSAL BROTHERHOOD OF MAN. I repeat the yoke shall be easy and the burden light. Many hands clasped together in the bond of love make what man of earth calls a task, a duty, well done. Bless you, Peace, Peace.

WHAT GOD IS AND HOW GOD RULES

Let there be no troubled hearts. Peace be still!
Though the sun has set beyond the horizon's edge
And darkness has found its way across the sky;
God lives and all is well. Peace be still!
The hearth is alive with the embers bright.
So let, within your temples, God's tapers flame
Light your path, Peace be still!
God lives and all is well;
Have no fret and neither worry
Nor in thought wonder. Peace be still!
Look not afar beyond for God, but know
That in your souls, His Light, His flame doth glow.
Peace be still and know that All is well
Live in light, the Light of God
As you now know him in your soul.
Let nought of mortal tongue in error spoke,
Disturb the peace within your soul,
God lives and all is well.
You sought Him at a distance, in error bound
And lo within your heart, He did abound,
Now in Truth, His Life, His Love, His Light,
His Truth you have found.
Peace be still. Peace be still. Peace be still!

My dear friends, you have separated the wheat from the chaff and you have not discarded the chaff. And so well must it be. For you shall return to look upon the vessel filled with chaff and it shall have turned to wheat, dear hearts. Let not your quest run with idle race. Be firm, unmoved and all that which in mortal reasoning, man says is impossible, you shall find it to be not so. All things are possible with God.

That which we leave with you in reference to Scripture is not idly mentioned. Would he who goes forth into battle, use a weapon and not know how to use it? There is no other manner to convince man

of his erroneous thinking than to show him the mortal discrepancy of
the weapon he has been using.

For eons of time man has referred to that which he has called the
Inspired Book of God. Man has become inspired to make records, and
he has recorded to the best of his ability and understanding. All that
which has been mentioned relative to God, contrary to the truth of
God-principal . . . Godman . . . God cannot be held accountable
for. Mortal man is a weakling in his mortal understanding. Godman
is not a power; GODMAN IS POWER and therefore MUST
NEEDS USE THE POWER, HE IS.

Let me repeat. There is nothing impossible with God . . . nothing
impossible with Godman. May I use man's term of speech . . .
mortal man's term of speech as you are familiar with it in the present
day? What a sad affair it would be if God were as man has been
taught to visualize him, in form, such as physical form, as you with
the mortal eyes see your physical form when you look at it in the
mirror. What a sorry state of affairs it would be, if God in such form
were limited to the degree of thinking and reasoning, that mortal
man is . . . and *there is the error.*

Man has not been properly taught, therefore man has conceived in
his thinking, that heaven is some far off place. May I say geographi-
cally located? And there upon a golden throne ascended by a wearisome, toilsome ascent of many steps . . . man meets his God with the
balm of Gilead in one hand and the sword of wrath in another. Such
has been the mortal conception of God. And such is untrue.

There is a Golden Throne, dear hearts and there is a power which
rules and reigns upon that Golden Throne and *that power is God.
The Golden Throne is within your soul's consciousness and the God
upon that throne is . . . principle.*

Listen with me! When man of earth thinks in terms of . . . God
PRINCIPLE INDWELLING . . . his physical body shall radiate the
beauty of the indwelling Principle . . . God. There shall be no worn
lines of distress in the physical brow, neither upon the countenance.
Man's physical step shall be quickened and no longer feeble and the
physical hand shall no longer tremble. For the inner radiance of the
living God shall have permeated every cell, every fibre, every muscle,
every tissue, every bone of the physical structure. The stooped shoul-

der shall straighten, the uncertain step becomes quickened, the dullness of eyes shall become bright, the physical deafness become sharpened with spiritual hearing.

Well did the writer of the Book of Ecclesiastes know, when he set in order acceptable words. Listen to them. They have no conflict with God, dear hearts. They are in accordance with the God which you now know. Listen to them, "Remember now thy Creator, in the days of thy youth," . . . the youth of spirit . . . and SPIRIT NEVER GROWS OLD. For as we have discussed with you . . . GOD IS BIRTHLESS. "Remember now thy Creator in the days of thy youth, lest the evil days come and thou shall say I have no pleasure in them."

As we mingle with mortal man we hear the cry of distress, the mortal cry, the mortal distress. We hear that which you call youth say, "Why was I born? I hate life! I wish I were dead! There is nothing for me to live for!"

Listen to the words again, "Remember now thy Creator in the days of thy youth." And the original statement said, "Lest the evil days come, when thou shalt say I have no pleasure in them, when the keepers of the house shall tremble." The wearing out of the nerve centers in the brain which govern the nerves of the body. The shaking of the arms and the legs . . . palsy, man of earth calls it . . . Nerve deficiency, says the diagnostician . . . general debility, says another wise man of earth . . . "When the keepers of the house shall tremble, when the grinders shall cease because they are few." The loss of teeth because of the lack of divine wisdom to take care of them. "And when they who look out through the window shall be darkened." The failing of physical eyesight, "And when the music in the streets shall become low." The deficiency in hearing, man of earth calls it deafness.

Refer back to one of our previous lessons, dear hearts, when we shared with you the words of Truth, that the physical body failed only because the centers in the brain governing the various parts of the body, no longer functioned properly. For eons of time man has heard of Faith healing, healing by prayer and the laying on of hands. Regardless of how the practitioner administers, *healing comes from within.*

When God reigns supreme upon His Throne, there is no confusion, there cannot be. Do not disregard God because man has misinterpreted God. You may call God . . . Him . . . He . . . She or Her . . . it matters not how you refer to God by name. BUT IN CONSCIOUSNESS, REFER TO GOD AS PRINCIPLE.

If mortal man would stop to reason how unfair he becomes in his judgment, in his criticism of his fellowman, he would have no argument with the God whom he has learned to revere or adore. For he could not expect any more from a God personal, than he could from himself, could he?

Mortal man is a lame, weak creature and he shall continue so to be until as those of ancient age who knew the Truth, worship God in Spirit and in Truth. Aramathrustra or Zoroaster, Confucius, Buddha, Amenhotep of Egypt and myriad other teachers, whom I could name to you, with whom by word of mention you would be familiar no doubt, *were all the incarnate Christ of God.* And unto men of their time in *their language, they gave to their peoples the Principle . . . God.*

What happens to your physical body when you devotedly and sacredly, with all reverence, intone the Sacred AUM of Life? Your very being becomes thrilled and enthralled. Why? . . . You are remembering your creator in your youth, for you are recognizing the birthless, youthful, indwelling healing, loving, Principle of the Universe . . . man has learned to call God.

A-U-M, three letters. T-A-U, three letters. G-O-D, three letters I-A-M, three letters. ALL MEANING BUT ONE POWER, dear hearts, God . . . G-o-d . . . G-o-d . . . infinite: All pervading, everlasting, undying, deathless Principle. Be not confused, be not confused, dear hearts. Whatever has served its purpose as you have travelled along life's path and you can no longer accept it in Truth, discard it. For again may I refresh you to one of our previous lessons, "Live not in the past, lest the dust of the past consume you. Render unto Caesar, that which is Caesar's and unto God that which is God's."

God can only do for man as man accepts God. Listen, dear hearts, listen to reason. As a man lives in his thinking, so he creates the path he travels. A peasant one time said to a very learned man who was about to forsake God because he did not understand God . . . I am mentioning no names, but perhaps the statement will sound familiar to you . . . the humble peasant said, "Foolish is the man who in mortal will thinks only of his body and disregards the richness of God." No truer words were ever spoken and to the one who listened, they became as a consuming flame. They set him in consciousness, on fire and he said, "Enough, enough, you have spoken enough. I understand!"

You will remember the sainted Augustine who said, "I have looked for you afar abroad and lo! Within my heart, I have found you." Listen, dear hearts. If there are those about you who are yet steeped in mortal confusion, remember a previous statement of ours . . . *do not measure yourself short by the yardstick with which you measure the shortcomings and discrepancies of your fellowman.*

I say this in Love, I have no quarrel. Cleave fast, hold tight with a firm everlasting grip to Truth as you have found it. For you are now . . . for you are now this moment, this very second, this very hour, facing in a direction which shall bring you into every freedom you have sought since your earliest quest . . . from the liberation of the bondage of confusion. Be still, dear hearts.

Upon the altar of your temple, in the presence of your God, Behold the lighted tapers of His Love . . . Be still . . . God lives and ALL is well.

Bless you, dear hearts. Bless you, Bless you.

I bid you a fond adieu.

CHEATING IN THOUGHT

How blessed is man in the sight of God. How glorified is man in the sight of God. His greatness is as great as his Creator and his glory is of the fullness of God.

Man's power is the power of God. Man's strength is the strength of God. *There is no weakness in man and there is no limitation.* Man is Spirit, the perfect image, the perfect likeness of God. Whatever imperfection there may be, is the imperfection of the flesh. As true as the words have been uttered, so it is. "The Spirit is willing, but the flesh is weak; many are called, few are chosen." Why should not all who are called be chosen? *Only that man does not choose to accept.*

Why the appearance of physical infirmity in the presence of the declaration of God's Truth? Why seeming continued infirmity? Why not an immediate response? Man, in his quest for health of body, peace of mind, success and abundance in all his affairs, too often is prone to forget and, in so doing, to look back.

How long has man lived in erroneous thinking? How quick does man change his thinking? Error exists only in the manner in which man expresses himself in his thinking. The more he thinks of God and his relationship to God, his true relationship, the sooner the desired results become manifestly evident, in his physical body and in all his affairs.

Quite frequently when man begins to forsake the old for the new, he hesitates and will say to himself, "Well, I will take a chance and indulge in a little bit of my old thinking. It shall not matter. I have yet time, I shall correct it soon, and all shall be well." And that is a mistake.

To he who becomes . . . shall I say . . . spontaneously divorced, instantly divorced, instantly separated from the mass race consciousness, making the declaration to be no part of it ever, and making that declaration in all sincerity; it is HE who is never prone to stumble or fall over the obstacles in the path caused by improper or erroneous thinking, before his desire to travel the path of Spirit.

Sincerity of purpose must become established. And when there would become an appearance of a recurrence of something of the old,

61

it is then at that time, that man shall remain steadfast, positive, in complete surrender, regardless of appearance. *God does not tempt his children.* God's children are prone to tempt God, and how does this happen?

Well, he who is not steadfast from the beginning is prone to say, "O, I shall leave this all to God. There is no longer any need or reason for me to be cautious or careful." And that is to be found particularly among those who are yet desirous of holding on to the old and tasting of the new; and I am speaking of their first attempt in changing their thought. "I can take a little chance; it shall not matter; God will forgive me."

My dear ones, there is no need for God to forgive, for God has never held man in account. God has never judged man. God has never suffered man's body to pain, nor has he suffered his coffers to be empty. God has not caused persecution, limitation. Therefore, man but tempts himself. And should man stumble and fall along the path in his pursuit of spiritual fulfillment, he neglects to look back to the time when he did a little cheating along the way.

Should there come a moment along or across the mystic's path when the clouds of distress hang heavy and low, let him take an inventory of his beginning when he first set foot upon the path of Spiritual enlightenment and let him say, "What have I done that transgression is now giving its appearance?

Medical science has declared that physical pain is nature's alarm clock, telling man that there is something amiss in his conduct, and that is well founded. But medical science fails to recognize that that, which is amiss had its origin in man's thinking. Error thoughts are not erased in the twinkling of an eye. Therefore, when one is in pursuit of spiritual happiness and there comes the appearance of physical distress, financial lack, or whatever it may be, let that one say to himself, "My prayer shall be more perfect. There is yet a little housecleaning of the old, of the past, it is not all gone."

There has been a statement made by many, "When man does not forget, he has not forgiven." And that can be well accepted, for unless man forgets ALL of the past, there is not room for complete forgiveness. Now remember, God has no reason to forgive. Man must forgive himself and man can only forgive himself his debt of the past . . . he can only forgive that debt and redeem that debt, by *completely forgetting.*

If there has been a habit, it must be erased. There is a danger in pushing it back into the thought chamber. For there it lays like the seed in the soil; and at some unguarded moment, a thought kindred to it, may be planted along side of it. Companion seeds are dangerous, therefore man must ever be alert to his perfect oneness with the perfect principle—God.

It is a very good mental exercise for man to indulge in during his last waking moments, just before sleep overtakes consciousness. And it is done in this wise, *"All of error which has surrounded me during my waking state is no part of me. I surrender to the fullness of God's pure, sustaining Love. I am his child and God is perfect."* Or words to that effect, thoughts to that effect. And should there be, perchance, some tiny, lurking, undesirable thought from some action or some attraction during the waking hours, it shall be eradicated. Memory is dangerous when memory is not sweet and pure.

Why does man, when he is seemingly sitting on the highest possible pinnacle of progress, find himself slipping and falling? It is only because, at some unguarded moment, even though it were a slighting, covetous thought entered his consciousness. And perchance he was totally aware of it at the time but said, "O, that little thought shall not hurt. I am strong enough to overcome that. I am close enough to God, that THAT little thought shall not matter." And that is dangerous. That is what may be called taking a chance on the losing side of the ledger.

We have used this illustration before. May we use it again please? Have you ever watched the tiny snowflakes buffeted about by the wind? Seemingly helpless little things, but one by one, they fell upon another. One by one they fall along side of another, and gather and gather, until at last in numbers they become veritable mountains; mountains of strength, blocking mode of travel, making it difficult for man to get about. Tiny little snowflakes, seemingly helpless yet together becoming a great power; tiny little thoughts, seemingly unnoticed. Thoughts with idle concern are like the tiny snowflakes, one upon another, one along side of another.

The humble Nazarene understood the power of thought for He

said, "If ye forgive not, how can your Father forgive?" That is a translation as you read it. But the humble Galilean made the statement in this manner, "If ye forgive not, how therefore can acceptance in forgiveness so become?"

You would not crowd a vessel from which you were eating with that which was unclean, for it would contaminate the food you had in the vessel.

I am leaving this lesson with you, dear ones, for the hour shall strike when someone shall cross your path and with complaint, perhaps, question. Therefore, it is expediently wise to have the proper answer at the proper time, in the proper place.

Our lesson at this moment is not in direct criticism of any one of you, dear beloved. But if you will contemplate the lesson it will prove to be of invaluable wisdom to you as you travel along the path of spiritual illumination.

Goodnight.

MEDITATION

Would you join us in a few moments of prayer and meditation?

As you become physically calm, center your attention toward the tabernacle of the Hosts by looking inward and upward and with a desire to behold the radiance of the *white light,* in the foremost part of your head; in the forehead, just above and between your physical eyes. You may not behold it immediately, it may take a little time. Whether it becomes a conscious realization to you or not, in prayer proceed in this manner;

I am now in the presence of Pure Being,
I behold no other radiance than the radiance of the Christ Light
Of which I am a divine part,
I am now fully conscious of the presence of the indwelling God.
I now behold the Living Christ of God, in whose image and like-
     ness I AM.
I ascend in consciousness and stand before the altar
Which I have created through my desire of oneness
With the Infinite Supreme Principle of the Universe,
That Principle which has brought all life into manifestation.
I am no longer part of doubt or fear,
I am at peace with all mankind through the Love of the Living God.
I behold nothing but perfection,
I see all mankind in perfect spiritual accord.
I proclaim peace on earth, as it is in Heaven.
Nothing can separate me from the Living God.
I send forth thoughts of Love to all those who may be
In understanding less fortunate than myself.
I bathe them, Spirit, Soul and body and see them continually bathed
With the Goodness and the Greatness of God's Love.
There is no confusion in the Universe. I see none, I hear none.
I hear but the voice of God and I feel the Presence of God's
Oneness throughout the Universe,
I see youth in all that which expresses Life, I see Life eternal.

I do not, I cannot behold or become a part, for myself or my
    fellowman,
Of that which man has learned to call death;
I see Health, Peace, Life in every full measure of abundance
Wherever Life is expressed,
I am one with the Living God; I see no defeat.
I do not know or understand what man has called annihilation.
Every good purpose and every good deed;
Every good act, every good thought, continues its growth
Throughout the Universe.
I am now in the Presence of Pure Being
And all of that which I shall ever become a part of,
Rests in the presence of Pure Being.
I know no malice, no contempt,
I am one with God and my fellowman.
So mote it be.

Dear Hearts, let this be your prayer whenever you are in meditation, whether it be for yourself or for others. Let it not be just idle
thinking but let it be thought with all the dynamic power within
your understanding. Be firm. Be positive, ere long at will, without
any forethought you will see not only within, but around about you,
the bright white light of the universal oversoul; that which man has
referred to as the universal cosmos.

Be faithful. Goodnight.

Peace, Peace, Peace.

GODMAN

Greetings; Bless you a thousand times ten thousand. Blessed is all mankind in the sight of God. Be fervent, loving, humble. Know that you are a child of God and there can be nought separate you. *There is no separation in God. God and man are one.* Man the perfect image and likeness of God; in Truth, in Pure Substance, in the wholeness of Life.

Had man been properly taught, man would not recognize the error of separateness from God. For you will remember the words of the humble Galilean when he said, "Though I am in the world, I AM not of it. I and the Father are ONE." And when the disciples marveled and the multitudes marveled in even greater measure, as to the manner of things which the Galilean accomplished; even before they voiced the spoken word he said, "Marvel ye therefore not at the things which I do, for even greater things than these shall ye do . . . for even greater things than these shall ye do."

His greatest command was, "Love thy neighbor as thyself." What in truth did the humble Galilean mean in that statement? Shall we consider it, dear hearts? "Love thy neighbor as thyself." When man has come into the realization that he IS the image and likeness of God, not created in the image and likeness, *he is the likeness.* When that becomes a conscious realization, day by day, hour by hour, moment by moment, with every breath he takes, he shall love God. And to love God is to love himself. To love God, to love himself, is to love his neighbor.

Jesus gave unto His disciples a prayer, a pattern of prayer and not only unto the disciples; but he passed it unto the multitudes and down through the ages it has passed on down to humankind and the opening statement is this, "Our Father, who art in Heaven, Hallowed be Thy name." . . . Our Father . . . God . . . Principle . . . Eternal Substance . . . Divine Mind . . . God in Heaven.

The Galilean likewise stated, "The kingdom of God is within you." And God is always in His Heaven. Therefore the kingdom of God, the kingdom of Heaven, are states of consciousness within the consciousness of man.

67

Would you ask me if there is a difference in man? My answer to you would be this. There is a difference between men but not with man. Remember dear hearts, remember M-A-N, man, G-O-D: both words three letters, and in God you have but one vowel. In man you have but one vowel and each vowel throughout the Universe from the beginning of time, as it is known through the Scriptures, has had the vibratory action of the power of six. Six symbolizes accomplishment through action.

So let us add the two sixes together of the O in God and the A in man and I believe you will agree that it digits a twelve. Is that right? And the one and the two of twelve are three. And three is the *triune principle, the indwelling deity God, man, Godman.* But it is not quite so with men.

Men for eons of time since the narrative of the Fall of Adam . . . so-called Fall of Adam . . . has been prone to live in digression of God Law. Why? For the reason that men are not, as an aggregate mass, God conscious. Why? For the reason that they have followed forms which, in time, become fables and fancies.

But Godmind is Godman and Godman is Godmind, and Godman lives by principle . . . the principle of the living God, the innate God. Not by form, not by fancy, not by fable.

When man has elevated himself in consciousness he is at one with God. And when man is at one with God, truly at one with God, sincerely at one with God, he can see but the Christ of God, reflected in his fellowman. Therefore, he can in Truth and earnestness pray that prayer, "Our Father" . . . ALL INCLUSIVE . . . "Our Father in Heaven." Then he is loving his neighbor as himself, he is loving his neighbor as he loves God.

If I may use the language of your day, God is not interested in tags, labels. God is not interested in denominations. God is not interested in creeds, as man has established them . . . or shall I say MEN have established them? *There is but one creed in Godmind and that is tolerance, brotherly love,* the Love of God beheld in all that which expresses life. Whether it stands upright and faces the sun, as your physical bodies do, or whether it creeps and crawls; whether it blooms in your garden or along your highways of Life, whatever expresses the Life of God is God's creation and Godman Loves all that which expresses life.

Godman is not interested in destruction. He is not interested in how he can cheat and take advantage of those with whom he lives. Whether it is in business dealings or otherwise, Godman is always willing to share. His hand is extended, palms up, and the palm filled . . . if you please.

Men . . . men . . . the aggregate mass . . . their thinking contaminated with the race consciousness, wholly unaware of the fact that they are living in the flesh embodiment for the reason that it is another opportunity to clear the error of the past.

Man should have long since known this Truth, had it not been denied him through ERRONEOUS TEACHINGS. I tell you dear hearts, life is everlasting. And when men of earth have cleared the record and no longer have a desire to return to a flesh habiliment, Life continues in the Celestial spheres which man has been taught to call Heaven. There man lives, no longer to become a denizen of the mundane sphere.

However, there is an experience which man may engage in, if in consciousness he so desires to do. And that experience he may have after he has left, lain by the wayside, the mortal coil which he once tenanted. What is this experience? In a moment of quiescence, my dear ones, have you ever felt the nearness of someone about you and perhaps you were alone in the room at the time? Have you ever had the experience as though someone had touched you or a breath, as it were had passed upon your cheek? Have you ever had the experience of hearing someone walk in the room and then said to yourself, "O, it is but my imagination."

Be not deceived, be not deceived my beloved. Life is eternal. Men of earth do not have the power to "call back" as the term is used, those who have dissolved the mortal coil. It is not necessary. For after man has left his physical body he returns at will.

Remember, beloved of the Fathers house, love cannot die. God is Love; God is birthless, ageless, deathless and likewise is man. I tell you, dear hearts, I tell you, . . . there is no death. Now then, should man after he has become dislodged from the mortal coil, with no longer a desire or necessity to return to it; should he so desire to project himself, that his beloved of the mundane sphere may see him . . . that is possible. Do not be deceived by what you might hear to the contrary. I tell you that is possible.

How is it brought about? In this manner. You will remember the words of the Apostle Paul when he said, "There is a natural body and there is a Spiritual body." So in thought, those who are dislodged from the mortal coil clothed that thought with the spiritual body, thus creating a likeness or a semblance of the physical body they wore when they were denizens of the mundane sphere of Life. In the fraction of a second, as you reckon time, it is possible for you to see it. Has it happened to you? Perhaps, for I am aware as I am visiting with you that there are those of you here, in this sanctum, who have had this experience. Be not disturbed by it. Do not anxiously covet it in the future. Moreover, be welcome in your thinking, be welcome in your thinking. At all times be ready to receive.

To those of you who perhaps have not yet had that blessed experience, likewise do not reach forth for it in covetousness; moreover say, "You are welcome, my dear one, you are welcome, in God's Love you are welcome." *The greatest power on earth is the power of love. There is no power greater,* dear hearts. I would ask you, to the best of your ability, in your quest toward the Father's House . . . to the best of your ability . . . learn to say; and as you learn to say, learn to mean, "I am at peace with man." And when you are at peace with man you shall be at peace with men.

What are you decreeing, what are you declaring when you say, "I am at peace with man." You are giving recognition in your consciousness that though man may err . . . as your man made society beholds error . . . though they may err, though they may bend and sway to unrighteous things, you are beholding the Christ of God in their consciousness. And I promise you, dear ones of earth, the more you declare love; the more you express love; the more you shall quicken the consciousness of those whom you meet, the Christ of God, which THEY are not aware of.

You have a sacred duty. The Love of God imposes no tasks, God is not a taskmaster. You shall never weary . . . you shall never weary . . . in service to your God. To the contrary, your experiences shall be happy. The distress of your physical body shall vanish. Should your eye be dimmed, it shall become bright. And should life have appeared to you as a problem, all that which has been problematic shall be dissolved, as your earthly snow dissolves before the vibratory action of the sun's rays. "I am at peace with man . . . I am at peace with man . . . I behold in those with whom I move, no evil. I behold the perfection of God. I bear no malice, I bear no hate, I see no confusion."

And when the opportunity presents itself for you to speak a word for the living God, as you learned to understand it, as it has brightened your path, do not hesitate to speak. But our word of admonition is this, dear children, NEVER PROSELYTE, NEVER PROSELYTE. Drop your seeds of Love as you walk along life's path. Drop them with a blessing. Water them with the waters of kindness and perchance should it so become your lot to meet those whom at one time you met in dire distress, you shall meet them with a smiling face, a quickened step, a song on their lips, peace in their hearts. "I am at peace with man and though I may be persecuted, vilified and cursed, I shall give love. For God has created and sustained in love and it is because I have found God's love that I am enjoying freedom, I share it with my fellowman."

Bless you, bless you a thousand times ten thousand, bless you, you are all precious in the sight and the presence of the Living God.

SEEDS OF CREATION

Greetings! Peace abide with you!

How good it is for brethren to dwell together in unity. Peace, Peace. As beautiful as your physical day is, so is the beauty of that portion of life's pattern allotted to you to live, in this present physical itinerary. The light of God's sun in your heart's consciousness shines. Let nothing obscure its radiance. As the reed in the marsh bends in the breeze, so let your life be ordered in Truth.

Wherever Truth is to be found, find it, and as the reed in the marsh bends to the gentle breeze, so in your heart's genuflection, bow in acknowledgment to Truth. Whether it is spoken across lips of the man whose skin is black, yellow, bronze or white, it matters not, so long as it is truth. In so doing, your message, as you deliver it, shall find favor.

There is but one door through which all man must pass and that is the DOOR OF TRUTH. Pass through it beloved, wherever and whenever you find it open. And should perchance, it swing closed and you know there is Truth dwelling behind that closed door, never fear to knock upon the door and arouse the Teacher.

The true disciple never tires in his quest and the Initiate is always gracious. The Teacher serving God and God Principle is never too weary and the hour is never too late. And, when the seeming stranger knocks upon your door and you have Truth to share . . . which you have . . . never say, "Come tomorrow, my time is now spent." Open the door and welcome the stranger. For as you seek to have your hunger satisfied, many you will find of like desire.

There are buried treasures to be found and man never becomes a pirate of the high seas to find hidden treasures. There is never a necessity for deception or theft, as the story of the pirate of the high seas relates. Earnest desire . . . Earnest desire shall open all closed doors and unlatch every concealed chest and treasure box. Let your desire wax, and as it does, you shall always find the oasis in which to dip your cup and quench the thirst of your desire.

Never forget the path of the past over which you have traveled to reach the height on which you now stand. Never forget that path, as you meet your fellowman of today, as you understand today, who is traveling a similar path.

As we discussed with you in a previous visit, *growth is ever necessary*. All nature goes through the experience of expansion and growth. Here, about your castle, as the warm rays of the sun kiss the earth, you shall plant seeds. You shall hold them in your hand, some very tiny; all similar in color, with a few exceptions, some larger in size; but dry seeds, dry shells. And as you place them between your fingers and with some manner of apparatus, or another finger, you make a tiny groove or a tiny hole and drop that seed. You then cover it over. You tuck it away to sleep and you wait, full well knowing that your efforts shall be rewarded . . . Remember all similar in color, with an exception of a few. But, within that tiny shell rests a heart. And after you have covered that shell, you do not see what takes place. What happens? Moisture and the warmth of the sun, cuddle, nurture the heart within that shell. Then that little heart begins to expand and soon there is no longer room within the little tiny shell . . . the shell bursts.

What has happened? Why does the kernel or the heart within that tiny shell expand? Only for one reason . . . *it is alive* . . . *it is a part of the great Cosmic mind* . . . Therefore, it has been but asleep and when quickened by the Power of God in action . . . it awakes! And here let me pause. I desire to refer you to the Fifteenth Chapter of 1st Corinthians, and therein you will hear the Apostle Paul speaking in this manner. He says, "And God hath given a seed and unto each seed a body after its own kind." God hath given a seed . . . not man. Read it . . . Ponder over it, dear hearts. It is there.

After Godmind has expanded in that tiny capsule or shell . . . what is the next act which your physical eye does not see? There is a tiny white tentacle or root which comes forth seeking moisture, seeking the Waters of Life. And, as it grows in length, there are other tiny tentacles which branch forth from it, seeking the Waters of Life . . . desire for further expansion and growth . . . you have learned to call them roots. What happens next?

Regardless of what appears above the soil, this takes place. A tiny sprout, always magenta in color, rises to the surface of the soil and from within that sprout comes forth a green sprout. What lesson have we to consider? All colors of the spectrum or the aura are contained in white, the pure white light of the eternal Cosmos . . . White, dear hearts, WHITE. Remember it.

What is the symbology of the magenta? It is the combination of the *highest pinnacle of life's polarity,* and the other extreme, *intelligence manifested in and through matter.* And for your growth I ask what combination of colors create magenta? Red and violet. And where do you find red and violet in the spectrum? One is on the cool side of the spectrum and the other is on the extreme opposite.

So, through the warmth of desire and the coolness of tolerance, you have magenta. Look at your rainbow, one of God's great expressions. Where do you find green? In the center of the spectrum. Out of the warmth of desire and the coolness of tolerance, come forth life. Always symbolized by green. What was it the dove brought back to Noah? It was the green olive branch which told Noah that life still existed. As the tiny green sprout grows, it sends forth branches and upon each branch, regardless of the species of growth, there are tiny buds. Some buds bear leaves, other buds bear blooms, and the leaves shelter the blooms and the blooms create fruitage.

On and on goes life, from the heart of God, bathed and sustained by the Power of the Eternal Cosmos. Call it what you will by any other name, it matters not. It is ever the eternal Cosmos . . . *God in action.*

Man who stands upright facing the sun, has yet his greatest lesson to learn, from that which he in mortal consciousness believes he controls, the lower forms of life. All man has to do is look about him and he finds at every turn of the road as he watches the response of Nature . . . he finds that there is another book, which he has not yet read. It is the UNWRITTEN BOOK OF LIFE.

Some of your mundane teachers refer to it as the Akasic record. Where is the midwife who assists the so-called dumb creature to deliver its young? Where is the midwife who breaks the waxen covering upon the bud of the tree and all other growth, to liberate the leaf and the bloom? There is but one midwife there and that is the great eternal midwife, the creator . . . God.

Beloved, you are beginning to read the unwritten records and as you read them and behold their beauty in all that expresses life, even rocks, for remember rock formation is not lifeless . . . nothing is lifeless. As you begin to understand man termed "wonders of nature" you come closer to your God; and you shall understand the capsule in which you live. You shall understand how, when the seed was planted in the womb and fertilized by the ovum, it expanded, how the tiny white tentacles sought the waters of life and how the warmth of desire and the coolness of Tolerance brought forth the magenta, from which came the physical body you now wear.

Again may I refer to the Apostle Paul, for the path he chose to trod was anything but smooth, and through the lessons he learned he was able to say to those who became destructively critical in their opinion, "Be ye therefore not given over to appearances, for hath not God written His Law in their hearts." That is sufficient. Man has coined this statement, "You cannot judge the contents of a book by its cover," and that, dear ones, you have proven to be true. Let us never be deceived by appearances. We of the council never permit it to be, out of all walks of life, the lame, the maimed, the halt, the tall, the short, the lean and those of flesh, those of all colors and races, we make our choice. Bless you, Bless you.

JUSTICE AND DECEPTION

It is always our pleasure to greet you and throughout the length and breadth of your land the harvest is becoming great, and the need of laborers in the field of harvest becomes so very necessary. Time is rapidly approaching when there shall be more questions asked than Orthodox Theology can answer.

In the very early Sixteenth Century a prediction was made—"Toward the close of the Twentieth Century all Religious Systems would have become numbered in the heap of discard and man of earth. through desire to know Truth, would make a demand." That demand is very close at hand.

It is needless for me to state or to remind you, that not only in the field of religious systems, but among the men who have been entrusted with the affairs of nations, are those not living true to their trust. There is no great mystery to that, for religious systems have caused man of earth to BECOME WEAK IN HIS UNDERSTANDING OF GOD; weak to that great task where he has discarded belief, BELIEF IN GOD. For that reason, spiritually and politically, the NATIONS STAND IN JEOPARDY.

There is a solution to the Problem and we seek mundane collaborators through whom we may pass the message of Spiritual emancipation. Mind you, we make no demand, ever, and we do not ask for those who represent us to resort to proselyting. You will find that the yoke shall be easy, and the burden shall be light. Mortal man who seeks to deceive his neighbor and all mankind of earth, become neighbor with neighbor. Though there be myriad in physical numbers, there is but one presence . . . *one presence . . . the presence of the ever living God.*

Therefore, regardless of how *one man attempts to deceive another, he but deceives himself.* It is unfortunate that man has become GODLESS to the degree that he is ready to sell thirteen ounces for a pound. But whom does he deceive? Judas deceived and, as the story is related, released his physical body from his soul. It has ever been thus and so shall it continue to be until man shall understand that salva-

76

tion is now. NOW is the day of salvation. It cannot be bought with thirty pieces of silver.

You will remember the story of the betrayal. Judas held thirty pieces of silver in a leathern bag and he held it in his right hand . . . thirty pieces of silver . . . three . . . *symbolizing his triune inheritance with the great oversoul of life.* And the naught of the thirty, the *all inclusiveness of which he was spiritually,* and the leathern bag, concealed the thirty pieces of silver. And thus man, within the treachery of his thinking, conceals his birthright. There are many a Judas, many a Thomas, many a Peter. Throughout the length and breadth of your land you will find many of such character.

Listen, dear hearts, the day of atonement is now. Now is the time for man of earth to make his repentance. Now is the time for man of earth to meet his maker. Not in the sweet bye and bye, for there shall be no sweetness in the bye and bye, if man carries the bitterness of gall with him into the bye and bye. For he shall find himself as he has so conducted his physical journey.

Let the waters of Mara be sweetened now, for there is no greater way in which for man to accomplish this, than through the law of justice. Each teacher in their time has taught the lesson of Justice. There is but one way and that is for man to be fair, upright, with his fellowman.

Dear hearts, do not worry because of the injustice dealt to you. Regardless of how unfair your fellowman has been with you, you are now looking at life, not through a glass darkly, but you are standing out in the open field. You have become monarch of all you survey.

Would you ask me, "What shall I do with that of injustice of the past?" My answer to you is this, "Cut it loose and let it go." For it shall find the womb from which it had its birth. You shall not have to direct its way. It shall find its own way, for remember . . . may I repeat a few words I left with you some time ago . . . perhaps they will become sweeter music upon your ears than when I first brought them to you. Listen:

"There IS part of the sun in the apple,
And there IS part of the moon in the rose."

God truly has put His Heaven into everything that expresses life. And the individual whom society brands the lowest of the low, is a part of God. His mortal cunning, his mortal treachery, may have obscured his vision of God, but he is God's child; and regardless of how cruel his conduct may have been, there is only one picture to behold and that is the innate dwelling Christ of God.

It shall spell freedom to you. It shall spell freedom for you. *Hold no man of earth in contempt.* Ever be free to say, "You are God's child." And, in your prayerful meditation, remember those who are less fortunate than yourself. Let your prayer of peace and love be universal, you are responsible to yourself. You are a child of the Living God. *Be there karma from age upon age, let not karmic debt trouble you, when you have learned to live in peace and freedom with your God.*

Man is responsible to himself and to himself alone. This I speak to you in Truth. Be not deceived. "Evil communications corrupt good manners," said the Apostle of ancient age. Be not deceived. Look not to any man-made ritual to absolve whatever misdemeanor has crossed your thinking. Such ritual, such does not exist. And I do not say this in any form of malice or ridicule. Do not be deceived.

Learn, dear hearts, to speak with a smile in your voice and, by no means ever, seek to bind your fellowman. With the same freedom that you would enjoy, render unto your fellowman that same freedom. In so living, there can be no accumulated debt or karma in that which man has learned to call the future.

If your fellowman would stand within your gate with his hands and feet seemingly tied and shackled, let your question be this, "What would I do under a similar circumstance?" Has your path ever been rough? Have you come to a place along Life's Path where your hands and feet have been manacled? Then you experienced release! Stop, contemplate your release and in prayerful meditation say to your brother, "I cut you loose and free you in the freedom, the allness, the oneness, of the Living God of whom we are both a part thereof."

This is salvation. This is being born again. Then you have a perfect right to say, "I am a *'borne again'* Christian in God. . . .

FULL AND COMPLETE SURRENDER IN HEART, dear one, shall never cause man to speak in terms of enmity.

Your name upon a scroll or roll, wherever it may be placed, is of no avail unless in spirit and in truth, your name has been inscribed upon the inner scroll, that scroll which is never scrutinized by physical eyes. Your name so placed, shall be recognized the length and breadth of the Universe. Then you can place your name to whatever man-made scroll may appear without fear of contradiction . . . *first within.*

The time is at hand, dear hearts, and it shall come to pass before your physical bodies have fallen away from your Spirit and Soul. It is rapidly approaching, when the prediction made in the early Sixteenth Century, shall be written across the length and breadth of the land. *Churchianity shall have ceased to be and Christianity shall come into full fruition.* Man can no longer deceive man for THE CHRISTIAN AGE IS AT HAND. Each tyrant, in their time, each dictator, as you have learned to call them, each individual seeking individual supremacy has but goaded man on to seek, to delve, to fathom, to uncover, until SOUL RESTLESSNESS IS BECOMING A DYNAMIC URGE, as it were.

And man is asking, "Why is this? Why has two thousand years and more of Churchianity failed?" You are coming into the possession of the answer. And our Council, unseen to human eyes, the members of which are myriad in number, are seeking mundane collaborators. For at long last a Spiritual Science must prevail and as the test tube in the laboratory reveals, that which the man of science seeks to find, so in your laboratory of thinking, you shall bring forth the perfect specimen in your spiritual test tube, please.

A hymn writer wrote, "Work for the night is coming." I say to you, "Work for the day is becoming brighter!" Man loses his way in darkness but he finds his path in the brightness of the Great White Light of Cosmic Principle. Let your labors be not in vain.

Bless you! Bless you! Bless you! Goodnight.

GIVING IN LOVE

Greetings! There is Peace, there is Peace. Proclaim it, dear hearts, Children of the Living God. There is peace. What man of earth can say there is no Peace? What man of earth can truly say, "I do not Love?" Let man be mindful of that which he Loves, for that which man Loves, he is a part thereof. For he has created that of which he is a part, in his desire.

Never let man utter the words, idly so, "I love this or I love that." There are many things along life's path man may be justified in saying, "I like," but let him be cautious how he shall use the word love. The word Love is POWER, therefore, man shall be mindful of that which he loves. Love is devotion. Unto what shall man ascribe his devotion?

Each teacher, in their own time, unto their own people, have said, "Be not given over unto false gods. There is but one God, the Creator of all that which is good." And, as you are acquainted with the Story of Creation, you will remember there were seven Steps in Creation, as you understand the Story. And Spirit . . . God said, "It is good." Then a pause . . . as you understand the Story . . . as we have in our previous visits discussed with you the Story of Creation. *Creation has never ceased.*

ALL man of earth continues to CREATE, and that which he creates is *his own* and no other man of earth has the power to take it from him. That which man creates, he gives, he shares, and in the measure in which he sends forth that which he creates, his well of Creation never becomes dry and parched.

What does man create? The word love expresses power, spiritual love, unselfish love. The love realized through the regeneration creates all of that which man can safely call good. There is an unregenerate love, dear hearts. You cannot love that in the physical which man knows as temporal for it shall pass away. It is your birthright to like it, and in a measure to possess it, but then too, man shall use it righteously. What had the Galilean to say of this? Did he not say, "Lay up your treasures in Heaven?"

Ah yes, we hear man of earth say, "I am going to have all of my good now, I am not going to wait until I get to Heaven." Well, there is no "good" for man other than the Treasures in Heaven, and as you already know from our previous visits, Heaven is a State of Consciousness. There lies your Treasure. Here, now, round about you, that is where your Love shall be centered, in heaven. It is an old saying and quite faithful and true that, "Man only keeps that which he gives away." Herein lies a seeming mystery. May we endeavor to share a few words of wisdom.

It is not within the law of God that man should live in poverty, destitute. It is God's Will that man shall have plenty, heaped up, pressed together and running over. I have no other word to leave with you than this, dear hearts, look within your own soul's record. Why have you prospered? Why are you able to share your goodly store with others? There is only one reason; it has been your desire to bring peace and happiness to your fellowman.

You, dear ones, who listen to me at this moment; you are here in this present flesh habiliment because, in your previous experience, you beheld the Light of Love, and as you may call it, circumstances, conditions of the mortal, hindered you from so fully expressing. Desire to express has brought you back into the present experience of Life's Eternal Span. Why comes to the door of your physical dwelling, your fellowman with a troubled heart, a throbbing breast, and a feverish brow? Why are you, dear ones, called upon to serve as Ambassadors of Peace, sharing your substance? As you sow in Love, share it. Desire, dear hearts, and you shall never be called upon because of the experience of desire to share that which is not yours to share. Your well of Love shall never become parched or dry and your physical resources, as you understand them, physically so, shall never experience poverty. This we assure you.

Remember the words passed to man for ancient age, *"The only thing a man shall keep is that which he gives away."* How can one continue to share were the well to run dry?

In your Holy Writ you read these words, "When you have it in your store, say not unto he who asketh of thee, come tomorrow." THAT IS DENIAL TO YOURSELVES.

Would you ask me this question . . . shall this be your question . . . "How shall I know when to give and when to share and when not so to do?" Listen, dear hearts, no one has ever come to you, and no one ever shall, only that one or ones who are worthy.

Here on your mundane sphere are countless numbers . . . and we speak not in the leastwise derogatory, please . . . who have full and plenty and unto whose door comes quite frequently one in need, but to receive this answer, "I can be of no assistance to you." And unto the one to whom the plea has been made, they live on in the flesh experience, adding unto what they have, wholly unmindful of that of chaos and strife around about them.

What does man bring into life, as man so says; and what does man take out of life, as man so says? And to that there is no mystery. Man brings into life . . . as he terms life . . . *every blessing he has ever experienced* and the results of every sorrow he has ever created. Therefore, the Nazarene knew when He said, "Lay up your treasures in Heaven, where rust doth not corrupt, moth destroy, and thieves break through and steal." The rust of selfishness, the moth of lustful desire and the thief of deception.

Love all of that which is good and be mindful never to say, "I wish I possessed that which he possesses. I love that which he has or she has. I would love to have that." Be mindful, dear hearts . . . covetousness never. Let your neighbor live with that which is your neighbor's, and thank God for that which is yours.

A duty never becomes a burden or a task, dear hearts, and love never becomes an imposition, never.

Always remember as you continue along life's path, as you are mindful now of the Truth, "It is not I who doeth the works, but The Father which dwelleth within me. Inasmuch as ye do this unto the least of these my brethren, ye do it unto Me."

If it is but a spoonful of cool water to parched lips . . . "It is not I, but the Father within me." Our blessings are with you. Become not weary in well doing.

The seven Steps of Creation are here represented in this hour. There are seven physical temples in this room and *ONE PRESENCE.*

Dear hearts, remember and never forget . . . as man of earth becomes a blessing, as he bestows a blessing, he receives a blessing. From the full measure of the heart comes forth the blessing. We have made mention of this many times. We refer to it now in particular because of the season of the year, which man of earth is about to indulge in and engage in . . . the season of the year of giving.

How shall man of earth engage himself or herself in giving? Shall it be with a freeness of heart? If so, be it a mite or a might, man becomes a blessing. How shall man indulge himself or herself in receiving a gift? Whether it be a mite or a might; lovingly, graciously, it shall become a blessing. Wherein lies the true value of giving, dear hearts? Is it weighed upon the balance with gold and silver? Ah nay, it is weighed with love. As God created and as God continues to create, does God become engaged grudgingly or out of necessity because of a particular season? How does man of earth indulge himself in the gift of God's Creation?

We so ofttimes hear man of earth say, "I have given lavishly but I have not received in lavish manner, hence, I shall give them no more lavishly until the gift has been recognized by some manner of equal return." And he or she who so engages oneself in giving, gives but to themselves a gift of limitation.

There is joy in giving for greater becomes man's expanse of living. O, the joy of giving! Greater is the living in the hearts of those who love. That is Heaven from above. Give and forget even that which you have given. Do not weigh it with Caesar's coin, for CAESAR'S COIN BEARS A TARNISH. It is well for man never to give, than to give and be boastful of the gift. Therefore, the Nazarene stated, "Where your heart is, there also shall your treasure be."

Likewise, said the Nazarene, "Let not, therefore, the right hand know what the left hand doeth. For your Father knoweth in secret or in silence and shall therefore reward thee openly." According to His richness, God's richness in Glory, shall your every need be supplied.

And the Apostle Paul, said in reference thereto, "Love vaunteth not itself; is not puffed up; doth not behave itself unseemingly; seeketh not its own."

It is better for man to scribe upon a tiny bit of paper these words, "I love you. God bless you," and give it in love than to give a costly gift in earthly gold and shout its merit from the housetop. Silently, lovingly, dear hearts, from out of the innermost depths of the heart, with no expectation of return . . . when there is no expectation of return . . . you shall have cast your bread upon the waters. They shall return unto you and you shall find them after many days, in the abundance of God's Law, God's Love, God's Light. Cut loose your gift and let it go. Bless your gifts.

Somewhere along the path the sun shall shine, a babbling brook shall sing, your parched lips shall be moistened. You will meet a smiling face. You will hear someone say, "My brother, my sister, I love you." And should the way become dark and should the coffers become lean, the bread cast upon the waters shall erase the leanness of the coffers. Have you ever experienced an unexpected blessing coming to you through an unexpected channel? Have you? If you have, why has it come to pass? Only for the reason that somewhere along life's path you became a blessing to someone . . . a blessing from the innermost depths of your heart.

Worry not. Rejoice! This shall be a happy season. And the season shall be as a seed, a fertile seed, planted in fertile soil. It shall grow, grow and grow, because you have given in God's Love with no expectation of return. Freely I give, freely I receive. *Receive! Accept! Appropriate in love!* As you send your gifts forth, bless them a thousand times ten thousand, for the joy that they shall bring in the hearts of the one who shall receive the gift. And your cup shall be filled to overflowing.

Bless you, Bless you, a thousand times ten thousand, Bless you.

WEAVING YOUR PATTERN OF LIFE

This is not an appeal to your curious thinking, for you are not curious, as man of earth is acquainted with the term. You are ready to receive. We have referred to visits of this nature as warranted errands. And you, dear hearts, are here in this sanctum, our sanctum, on a warranted errand. Worry not your hearts, become not troubled. Life has smiled most beautifully upon you.

We are aware of the rough places in your path over which you have crossed. *Look not backward.* Moreover, fix your vision upon the Star in the East for it shines. And within your Soul's consciousness there is a manger, and in that manger lies the wise man of old, the Christ of God.

You have conceived and given birth to the Wise Man, and the three who knelt at the manger in adoration have left their precious gifts and gone their several ways. But the greatest gift is in your possession. Accept it, cuddle it, nurture it, suckle it well with your love. May I repeat the words of an ancient wise metaphysical poet in the following words:

> "Would you know life abundant,
> Love doubled for all it gives?
> There is no means surer
> Than helping someone to live."

As you continue along life's path, clasping the hand of your fellowman, and as a statement is made, "Brushing shoulders with them," look for but one thing in your fellowman, the innate Christ of God. And you shall learn to behold the Christ regardless of the raiment which clothes the physical coil, regardless of whatever manner you may meet your fellowman.

You shall learn that God is Power, God is Love, God is Health, God is Strength, God is All Abundance. *You shall only find yourself in physical want because you have failed to nurture the Fourth Wise Man, the Wise Man in the Manger. Your Consciousness is the manger, dear hearts, and therein lays The Christ. Do not crucify your*

85

Christ. There is but one Golgotha's tree, dear hearts, and that is the physical body. The other tree upon which the physical man Jesus hung, has passed into its nothingness.

The manner in which you conduct yourself physically shall be in response to the manner in which you think. But would you ask me, "Why is it, I have to the best of my ability been kind, good? I have endeavored to live a clean, righteous life?" And that question is justified.

The humble Galilean was encountered by a very wise man, and the wise man said to the Galilean, "What is required of me to inherit the Kingdom of God? Tell me, O Good Nazarene."

And before the question was answered the Nazarene said, "Why callest thou me good? There are none good but the Father. Yea, not even I, but the Father which dwelleth within me."

The good of the Father, beloved, is you. You are the good of the Father. And EVERY priceless possession of the Father is yours. You are the Christ of God incarnate. Forget it not. Now, why have seeming troublesome times confronted you? Why have you met with individuals whom you would say have caused you grief and remorse? Life is endless . . . truly it is eternal. It is not a part of the Divine Idea that man should choose another physical form through which to pay his debts. That but happens through man's choosing.

Likewise the humble Galilean made the statement, "Now is the accepted time." Likewise He said, "Is not a thousand years likened unto a day and a day likened unto a thousand years?" And the Universe in which you live, The Father's House, has stood longer than a thousand years, yet but one day. Likewise the humble Galilean said, "Sufficient unto the day is the evil thereof." And Orthodox Theology has misinterpreted, distorted, the words of Truth which fell from the lips of the Galilean. Therefore he became provoked to say, "What man is with honor in his own land, in his own country?"

Today is the day. That which you call yesterday is but a memory and that which you look forward to as tomorrow, becomes today. Let memory be sweet, wholesome, constructive. For man is as a weaver standing at the loom of Life. Be mindful, ever mindful of what you put in the shuttle as you pass it back and forth. For you are weavers, weaving a pattern. Life is full, but unto each individual, by the individual's choice, is given a portion of the great patterns of life to weave.

The masses have never been reconciled to the fact of rebirth. But again let me take you to the words of the humble Galilean when he said, "Ye must be born again." And the counselor of law who stood before him, answered saying, "How can I a man grown, enter for the second time into my mother's womb and be born again?" And the Galilean said, *"I speak of the birth of the spirit."*

Now, that statement has been confused by Orthodox Theologians for they are not yet agreed upon the fact that Spirit is Birthless.

What could the humble Galilean have meant when he said, "I speak not of the birth of this flesh or the present habiliment," which the wise counselor was wearing, but He said, "I speak of the birth of the Spirit. Ye must be born again." And theology has said, "Only through religious rite and ritual, by confession of faith, can man be born again," and *THAT IS ERROR.*

It is as a smoke screen of doubt between man and his God. What happens with man? Why does his path cross the path of others, where he encounters seeming disagreement? He is meeting Caesar with whom he dealt in previous embodiment and mind you well . . . Caesar shall be paid, when Caesar is met. God makes no demand. What shall man of earth do when he encounters a fellowman who creates a seeming distress? He shall bless the fellowman and say, at least in thought . . . not necessarily in words of mouth . . . he shall say, "You are my brother, you are my sister, come up higher."

When is man's physical travail to end? When through desired consciousness, he completely surrenders in recognition of the indwelling Christ. Heaven is a state of consciousness and cannot be otherwise. And its opposite, call it perdition, call it gahena, call it hades, call it hell, call it what you will, is likewise a state of consciousness.

Man's tenanting a physical body is of his own choice, and not a mandate of God. In your scripture you read of the twelve thrones upon which man shall rule, as he follows the Christ illumination through the regeneration. Likewise, you read of the twelve portals of twelve gates to the Heavenly estate. And in the Zodiac you have twelve houses, do you not? And in which house does man start his earthly travail?

In the Zodiac we shall reason that Pisces is the first house. And rebirth after rebirth, after rebirth, after rebirth, man passes through one house to another, until he has come back to Pisces. And as he is journeying through the twelve houses of the Zodiac, he is ascending through the twelve thrones or centers of the regeneration and he is passing . . . if you please . . . through the twelve portals or twelve gates of Heaven. And this is all in consciousness, dear hearts. This is in accordance with Divine Idea. Your God is a merciful God, yet man in his ignorance shall say, "Why has God permitted this to have fallen to my door?" Do not blame God.

Now, you are justified in asking me this question, "Is it necessary for man to pass through the twelve houses or the twelve signs of the Zodiac for completion of Karma?" And my answer to you without the slightest hesitation is, "No, it is not." *As soon as man recognizes that he is in error,* whether the error gives its appearance through the meeting of confusion at the hands, so called, of some fellowman, or otherwise, let him say to himself, "There is something wrong here."

Likewise was the Galilean provoked to say, "Come, let us reason together." He was not referring to groups or multitudes of people but he was referring to the reasoning, *THE DIVINE REASONING OF SPIRITUAL MAN WITH THE MORTAL MIND,* as the Apostle Paul referred to it . . . or carnal mind.

You speak of certain planets in the ascendant. Where are these planets found in Truth? Well, they are found in Consciousness; each planet with which you are familiar is a state of consciousness. And those which are in the ascendant are the result of rectified errors through previous incarnations. And those which are . . . would you say . . . retrograde, or on the counterclockwise of digression . . . are debts which have not yet been redeemed.

We are aware that you are interested in a most interesting Spiritual Science. You call it Astrology. Please define the meaning of the word Astro?

Student: "The astral shell made by man's thinking."

And how comes the astral shell or astral body?

Student: "In man's thinking."

Every thought contrary to Truth, every deed as a result of every contrary thought builds this astral body. It is not strange that there is a kindredness of affection between certain men and women of earth. Desire brings it in to rebirth. It is not strange that there is a willfulness and an antagonism likewise. Desire brings it through rebirth and so the treadmill of life is endless until man finds Truth and it shall never be found in that which man has learned to call churchianity. *It can only be found in the higher precepts and principles of Christianity.*

What is Christianity? It is void of form. It never becomes a fable. It does not give its appearance as a phantom. Christianity is living the Christ principle, the wise man in the manger of consciousness in action and it meets you through every house of the Zodiac and through every experience.

Hurry and find it, dear hearts. Do not be concerned with that which spells digression. Be shut of it! Be clear of it! Say, "I had enough of you!" And all that you find in the ascendancy say, "You are mine, you have been with me from the beginning, but I could not see you because I was interested in fear, trouble, worry."

Planetary signs understood never become cumbersome weights. A writer with whom you are familiar, or rather his writings said . . . and it was Sir Francis Bacon who made the statement . . . "All that which is wrong, is wrong as thinking makes it such." And if you are going to hunt for signs and digressions you will find them. Seek, search, find, knock, and the door shall be opened unto you . . . ask, and ye shall receive.

Dear hearts, listen with me. You have espoused a precious science. It is of the Christ. It is Spiritual. It spells unadulterated, uncontaminated, Christianity. And, should you find one who is less fortunate than yourself, as you are making a delineation of their life, put your one hand on their shoulder and with the other hand grasp their other hand and say, "Come, you are my brother, you are my sister. Come up higher, we are one." Remember as true, as the statement has been made, it is, "God is no respecter of persons." And you, each one of you, are a Child of God from the very beginning, as man reckons time, millions of years ago.

Do not be deceived. Ritual, form, confession of faith, does not make you a child of God. You are God's child from the beginning of time and it shall ever be thus.

Bless you, bless you, a thousand times ten thousand.

Truly this is as the wedding feast of Cana; the wedding of the forces, rising from the Immortal Intellect to Spiritual Intelligence, Spiritual Substance. In the twelfth chapter of the First Book of Corinthians, the first book so called . . . you will find statements relative to the gift of the Spirit. And as you read those statements, you will find that there shall be those given over to the speaking in unknown tongues.

But the Apostle Paul says, "What shall it benefit a man, if they remain uninterpreted?" This next statement I make in love, in the fullness of love, and by no means in the leastwise in derogatory mention of that which man has engaged in, relative to the speaking of tongues, because of his misinterpretation. What is meant by the speaking in unknown tongues?

Are terms of truth recognized to those who do not understand? For you will remember that when the Apostle Paul wrote those statements for the peoples of Corinth, they were steeped in pagan superstition. And the unknown tongues, Paul referred to were the TONGUES OF WORDS OF TRUTH.

As we look back as it were, upon man of earth, and yea in this very hour, we find him wandering about on the highways or byways seeking, seeking, seeking comfort for mortal distress.

It is blessed, blessed indeed that you, dear hearts are joined together in this hour. If these words were to be heard in many of the places where man is now seeking release from the self-inflicted mental torment because of his unknowing, he would reject them. And we speak these words, dear hearts, without condemnation; for we come in love.

WHO IS TO BE CONDEMNED BECAUSE HE DOES NOT UNDERSTAND? Moment by moment, hour by hour, day by day, week by week, month after month and year after year, as you have learned to reckon time, man gradually seeks Truth and eventually he finds it. Blessed is the supreme idea of the Father, which has established the law of rebirth. While man of earth denies it, because of his ignorance of it, does not mean to say it is untrue.

Why are you gathered here this evening? It is not out of curiosity. It is not out of idle curiosity, but you, the image and likeness of God, you are beginning to travel back to the Father's house. You are willing to listen to "Unknown tongues." Unknown to the average individual, but not unknown to you. Why? For the reason that the involution of the Soul cries for the liberty it denied itself, when you are in adherence to, as in theology we used to say, "The Faith of the Fathers."

There can be no evolution to the flesh without involution, dear hearts. Now I may digress just a wee bit. Man has been prone to stand before a mirror and say, "Well, I look pretty good today," or to the contrary he may say, "I do not look so good." And that is error. For that which is seen reflected in the mirror, is not man. Here in this room as you look at the artificial light, you are seeing one of the myriad forms of electricity. But it is not the power. It is one of the myriad expressions of that power.

As you walk along the road you will see a tiny flower, a blade of grass, a reed in the marsh, gently moving; touched by the docile breeze. But let that which you have called the wind, gain in velocity and it no longer remains docile; but it becomes what you have learned to call a cyclone, a tornado. It causes the great typhoons and is capable of devastating great areas.

Have you seen the Power? I dare say not. *When man shall see God, he shall see himself and not until then.* And when in spiritual enlightenment he meets himself, he shall have met THE MASTER OR ANCIENT AGE . . . THE MASTER . . . THE WISEMAN . . . THE CHRIST OF GOD . . . born in the infant body. All birth of flesh is immaculate, dear hearts. It cannot be otherwise, for God is immaculate.

That which is conceived in the purity of thought, attracts the ancient soul coming back to claim one of its last physical habiliments . . . sex the greatest institution in the creation of the Father and the most sordidly abused.

Mary, who bore the physical body tenanted by the Christ of God . . . immaculate conception? Yes, dear hearts, and do not reject it. How came it about? But in this wise. Through THE BLENDING OF THE AURA, and that man needs to learn much about.

Why do you feel uncomfortable in the presence of certain individuals? Whether you have so stated or not, I dare say you have heard others make this remark, "I felt so uncomfortable when I was in their presence." Then, to the contrary, you meet individuals . . . as you call them . . . who, upon first meeting, you can safely say, "I love them, I cannot wait until I meet them again." And as your days roll by in the interim of another meeting, your soul yearns for their nearness. What has happened?

Well, to he who has traveled through many embodiments, the auric vehicle becomes refined. May I use that word? And when that individual meets one who has NOT passed through the *regeneration of the mortal will, there is a clash and hence no agreement; a disagreement*. But when two souls meet, vibrating on the same rate of Spiritual frequency . . . may I say, well, that is quite different. There is an agreement, there is an accord, there is an understanding.

You have come in contact with people and you have said to your self and to others no doubt, "I know them but I cannot remember where I have met them," and from then until now you are in a state of wonderment, as it were. Yes, you have met them, you know them. But why the seeming lack of recognition? Well, it is in this wise . . . *the recognition is soul recognition, the blending of the auras, the agreement, the accord.* The lack of recognition is because you are looking at the physical body, with the physical eye and of course you have never met that soul in that body.

Do not be disturbed. Do not become disquieted because you do not immediately recognize; but in the inner recesses of the soul's consciousness *WILL TO KNOW*. Man must pass through various devious experiences, and you are going through school again. You have passed through the same school many, many times, but through mortal confusion, you have failed to remember. But, dear hearts, as you become less desirous of the baser environments of the physical, is proof sufficient that you are reaching that state of soul growth where the veil shall be rent in twain and you shall remember all things which have ever been.

The Apostle Paul put it in these words, "When I was a child I spake as a child, I thought as a child; but when I became a man I put aside or I put away childish things. Now though I see through a glass darkly, then shall I see face to face." This is a very great step for you, dear hearts. And though you may be enthralled to a degree, and although you may question . . . which is your birthright . . . never accept anything until it becomes reasonable to you in consciousness. But whatever is happening in your thought process at this moment, give it room, do not annihilate it, give it room.

For you will remember, when the voice spoke to Mary she pondered the words in her heart. And as you ponder truth in your heart, you are bringing about the immaculate conception and you are making way for a new experience. This that you are indulging in, is not an accident. It has not come about by chance. It is the working out of the *immutable law of life.*

I trust that we have shared with you from the Manna of Life and the Manna shall no longer be hidden; but it shall be before you, ever in readiness for a feast, every moment of every hour of every day.

Remember, dear hearts, whatever you enter into to do, let this be your statement of Truth, "this I do unto the Father." Your hands as you stretch them forth are symbols of giving and as you close them and bring them close to your body, they are symbols of receiving. They carry either a benediction of love or that which is contrary.

Dedicate your body to the Father. Have no fear, dear hearts. Learn to say, "Use me Father for the purpose for which I am a part of your Eternal Creation." God is Love. His Heaven is your Heaven. It is within you. You have never been separated from God, *you cannot be separated from God, only as you so will to do in your disregard of the presence of God in your thinking.*

Truly this hour is as the Wedding of Cana. For the Bride and Groom have met. Intellect rises to intelligence and Supreme Substance . . . Infinite Being is the priest and witness to this marriage. We Bless it. We Bless it. We Bless it. Go forth in Peace. ALL of the Father's is yours and all that which you are and ever shall be is of the Father.

Our blessing rests upon those, who out along the highways and byways of life, are misusing their bodies. Listen, dear hearts, you may become Ambassadors of the Father. You may carry the message of Truth to those who are less fortunate than yourself. Do not scatter it in a promiscuous manner. But when the knock comes upon the door of your heart, when the inquisitor stands at your door, open it. For remember, the door to your heart opens on the inside. OPEN IT. Remember, regardless of how man has desecrated himself in the abuse of his talents, he is your brother.

You are the lights of the world. Your eyes have become singled unto the light. Therefore, dear hearts, the light is great; and how dark can the dwelling place of mortal man remain, when the light of God is shed within it. Let your light shine. Now one last word, you remember the Nazarene left these words, "And 'I' . . . listen, dear hearts . . . mind this well . . . and 'I,' if 'I' be lifted up 'I' shall draw ALL mankind unto me." You are the "I am," the "Christ" of God, incarnate in the flesh.

It was the Christ power, the Christ consciousness, which spoke through the physical vehicle of He who was known as Jesus of Nazareth. The Christ of God speaks through you, regardless of the circumstance, regardless of the condition which you meet, regardless of the individual you meet.

Learn to say this; "I behold you a child of God. The Christ in me greets the Christ in you." This is truth, dear hearts. God is no respecter of persons. You are His child. Your hands express, let them express Love.

We are grateful to you for your attention. We shall be with you again. Bless you. Bless you. Bless you a thousand times ten thousand.

So mote it be.

AN ASCENSION IN CONSCIOUSNESS

We are happy, inasmuch as you are making discoveries. And the greater the unveiling in consciousness, the sturdier your growth. Though it may appear to you that we speak in mysteries, it is not such. All that is necessary is for you to listen. And true to the statement, silently you ask. Of whom do you ask? Not we of the council. For in silence you are opening the door to the nearness of the vastness of which you are a part. What happens when you do this? You are experiencing the *ascension after the crucifixion.*

What do we mean by the crucifixion? You have, so to speak, crucified the five physical senses of their betrayals. You have not annihilated them, but you have eradicated betrayal. You are no longer a doubter. You are no longer a Judas, a betrayer. You are no longer an unregenerated Peter, a denier.

The three (moral perceptions) I have just referred to are three of the five physical senses which are most detrimental to man. And after you have crucified their deception into its native nothingness, you arise and begin to shine, as it were, in the fullness of the Great White Light.

All distress of the physical body, as we have previously mentioned, is because of imbalanced chemistry . . . chemistry! Is there anything which expresses life where chemistry is not to be found? We are agreed that in all that which expresses life there is to be found a chemical analysis. Although man of earth may not be agreed, we are agreed and as that which you have learned to call time unfolds itself, you too shall be agreed.

All life . . . all life wherever you find it expressed . . . cannot continue without light and color. For when all color is blended together it expresses its parent, The Great White Light Of The Cosmos. When man has risen above or ascended above worry, anger, fear . . . all that which is contrary to Love . . . let me repeat, when man has made the ascension and through knowing, through acceptance, declares his oneness with the Living God, each throne center, of which there are twelve, becomes radiantly active with the parent light.

95

In a previous lesson we referred to man in quest of Spiritual emancipation as being Israelitish. An Israelite is one who seeks release from bondage. You will remember the story of the Israelites as they were captives. They were held in bondage in consciousness. But, there was a man called Moses, and Moses led the children from Egypt.

What is the meaning of Moses? Emancipator, deliverer. And there was a parting of a body of water, as the story is told . . . Red Sea. What does the Red Sea symbolize? Why the Red Sea? It symbolizes Love. And at what particular season of the year did Moses lead the Israelites? It happened in the spring of the year meaning new life, new expression of life, all that which lay dormant during the season you called winter. And there is a portion of the spectrum of the sun which man refers to as cool or cold.

When man is wilfully disobedient to God he is in the winter season of life. He is not experiencing the warmth of love. But when the warmth of the spectrum kisses the earth, the bloom on the apple tree comes forth and, because of its obedience to the warmth of God Love, it becomes the apple . . . "part of the sun in the apple."

We have heard it mentioned that corn grows at night. Why does it express growth at night? Because there is part of the moon in the corn as well as the rose. And what is the Moon? The reflected light of the sun, and there would be no reflected light if it were not for the sun. Here is a seeming mystery to man. The rose like the corn is active because of the reflected light of the sun. It receives its beneficence during the day. But when the intense vibratory action of the sun's rays become less intense, as that which you know as darkness appears after that which you call the setting of the sun has taken place, the corn and the rose express in the quietude, listen, dear hearts . . . in the quietude, what they have absorbed when the sun's rays were very active.

"Out of the Vast comes Nearness." When man becomes mentally quiet, peaceful . . . call it meditation, call it prayer, call it what you will . . . when he removes himself from all mental frustration he becomes as the corn, as the rose. "A little bit of God's Heaven in everything that grows."

Man is inclined to become . . . and I want to be kind in making this statement . . . he becomes a trifle unmindful of God when everything about him appears to him to be beautiful. He is inclined to rather forget. He is like the mariner of old; when the sun shone bright and the sea was calm, the mariner became vicious with his seamen, blasphemous, tyrannical. But, when the sea became tempestuous and raged, he said to those with whom he had quarreled when the sun shone brightly, "Let us pray. Let us ask for a stilling of the waters, and to reach harbor safely."

And the voice answered him and said, "If you had found me in the calm, you would know me in the storm." The corn, the rose, found God in the calm of the day. And as the sun reflected its light to the darkness of that which man knows as night, the corn and the rose have no fear. There was no storm, no tempestuous sea.

What happens when imbalanced chemistry begins to express itself through the evidence of that which is known as pain, discomfort? That is the tempestuous sea. What happens when man seeks God? How is the sea calmed? How is pain annihilated? How does the physical temple become whole? Man, through prayer, desires to know God in greater measure though he has erred, speaks to each fiber, each cell, each particle of the physical temple; and particularly does he speak to the red and the pale purple corpuscles. And through quiescence, prayer, meditation, he becomes part of the vastness. He becomes peaceful. And though he is aware of it or not, he is saying to the corpuscular structure of the blood "Agree with thine adversary while thou art yet in the way with him." Become harmonious, ye laborers in the field of the Master, ye laborers in the vineyard of the Master. Work together in harmony. It has not been too long since we have said to you, harmony is borne from the womb of love.

Listen, dear hearts, wherever you see the expression of adversity as you walk along life's path, pause long enough in your thinking to say, "Father I thank you that that which I behold about me has not come nigh my dwelling." It has been truly written and truly mentioned, man's extremity becomes God's opportunity, and it has not been too long since we have spoken to you, dear hearts, OF FULL SURRENDER IN LOVE.

"Out of the vast comes nearness." All one, dear hearts, that is nearness . . . NOT ALONE . . . ALL ONE!

"For the God of Love, of which man sings,
Has put a little bit of his Heaven
Into every living thing."

And, as you ministered you became vibrant, alive, living, full, whole, from the storehouse of the Great Vastness of Infinite Supply. Another poet having read those beautiful lines of Love, expressed it in this manner:

"Would you know life abundant,
Love doubled for all you give?
There is a means no surer
Than helping someone to live."

Goodnight. Bless you, bless you, bless you.

WORSHIPING FALSE GODS

Life is a quiet stream of water. All is well. Do not look upon, nor accept the reflected confusion of he who has not the place wherein to put his trust. There is an hour which comes to he who is unconcerned with the true pattern of life. Moment by moment, hour by hour, man becomes closer to the realization of his kindredness to God. There are seasons when man is prone to wander from the path; some call it carelessness, others call it disobedience. It comes about through the creation of a false image. It is true that there is nothing impossible with God.

One of the ancients has said, "Thou shalt not take the name of the Lord thy God in vain." And man has been led to believe that taking the name of the Lord in vain is but desecrating God's name through speech. Likewise, it is written, "Thou shalt have no other God before me."

Taking the name of *God in vain is speaking in terms of limitation, thinking in terms of limitation, living in a mental atmosphere of limitation;* all that which is contrary to truth and justice between man and his neighbor. All manner of covetousness *is a part of false gods.* It is Truth profound that man attracts unto himself that which he desires. Worshipping false gods is placing error before truth, hence the statement, "What shall it profit a man if he gain the whole world and lose his soul?"

As we have attempted to reason before, MAN HAS NO SOUL. HE IS A SOUL. Therefore, to lose his soul is to lose himself. The man or woman who chooses to follow a certain desired pattern in life, should be content to go forth in the field of their labor and garner that which has been sown, but that does not happen. In the hour of desperation such a one cries, "O God help me!" And it is wise, when man finds the fruits of that which he has sown disquieting, that he becomes mindful to say, "God deliver me!"

There are some however, who, with a sense of false mental stability, here in the hour of darkness, continue to worship their false gods. And when the mixture becomes separated, the falling away of the mortal coil from the soul, they pass on into what man has learned to

call eternity . . . self-willed . . . still denying the creative principle
of life. Such a one does not return as readily as one who has accepted;
and in the interim between that what man has learned to call death
and rebirth, they continue to disregard and will not accept the LES-
SONS OF THE MASTERS.

What manner of path can such a one choose upon their return to
the earth plane? Only that which they have created . . . *man cannot
disregard the law of attraction.* You are wondering at this very
moment why we speak in this manner. Well, there are those myriad
in number who are waiting to return and we of the Council labor
with them zealously. But you may say to me, "If they will not
understand, why continue to labor?" Though they do not accept,
freely accept, yet there is a picture which they behold that cannot be
disregarded. And by the very law which they have established, which
shall bring them back into a path of like attraction, the picture which
has been created will reveal itself at certain intervals, after they have
started their trek along the physical plane of life.

Man cannot truthfully say that he lives in ignorance of Truth.
Man cannot say that. For each time he is prone to misbehavior, a
picture of Truth is revealed to him. And from memory's scroll he
reads the records of the masters of the spheres and he says, "I should
not do this. It is wrong."

If you were to ask him how he knows it is wrong, he perchance
would be unable to tell you. Yet the Truth becomes indelibly im-
printed. Thus we can be perfectly agreed that no man walks in total
darkness. There is a light regardless of its seemingly feeble flame.
Some call it conscience. That is a very good name. Others refer to it
as the still small voice from within, and that is expressing it most
perfectly. *The voice of the masters of the spheres speak.* Truly it is
the still small voice from within . . . memory . . . the voice of
memory.

Man cannot excuse himself from his error. He has, as you of earth
would say, no legitimate excuse. Man lives deliberately so. And in
Truth he cannot deny it. Each step along life's path is deliberately
taken. For remember, when man says in his thinking, "This is wrong
but I shall do it anyway." That is deliberate, is it not? Therefore, let
man be honest with himself.

Before leaving you, may I share with you these last words, will to live justly, uprightly. Continue to declare, "I will to live according to the perfect pattern." In so doing there is no room for error. It cannot enter.

Regardless of what you hear, do not become frustrated or over-wrought with undue anxiety. Constantly affirm, "I will to live in accord with life's perfect pattern." In so doing, it shall never become necessary for you to say, "I trust I shall be fairly dealt with." There is never any reason for man to deny error if man does not recognize it. Therefore continue to say, "The perfect pattern, the perfect will, is now manifesting itself in my life in all of my affairs." See perfection, think perfection, live it with every breath you take.

Should there come to your attention unkind statements, do not even take time to say that they are untrue. Continue to repeat, "The perfect will, the perfect pattern governs my life and all of my affairs," and in so doing you become no part whatsoever of adversity. You are listening to the still small voice of the great angelic hosts of the spheres.

Each night; particularly when you are lying your physical body down for its needed rest, as sleep overtakes your mortal form, drift out over the peaceful ether waves with this thought in mind: "All peace is mine. I share love with everything there is in life."

Do not say to me, "Can I truthfully say this?" Do not make that statement! Yes, you can truthfully make that statement. You can make it . . . mean it . . . live it. Each one of you can.

And in the morning, as you return to your physical temple to raise it from its couch of rest, stand erect, lift your head high, stretch forth your arms and say, *"All of God's perfect kingdom is mine. All of love is mine. All who love are mine, for I know nothing but love."* And let that be your thought throughout the day. And in so doing, in due season, as the blacksmith turns the piece of molten steel in the particular pattern he so desires to shape it, you shall have placed in order your house, your temple, your affairs. You shall have melted, as it were, hearts of stone.

What else shall you accomplish? Well, it is blessed, for your thoughts of love shall blend with our thoughts of love. And to those in need, you shall be tearing down for them some of the phantom gods they worshipped when they were in the flesh. Truly, truly, truly, the statement is profitable, overcome evil with good. Let your light shine, each one of you, let your light shine. Let your last pleading thoughts be of love. Let your awakening thoughts be of love. Let your thoughts during your conscious hours be of love. And when sleep has overtaken your physical body and you are traveling across the ether waves of eternal Life, you shall meet with no other force or power than love.

Goodnight.

TOUCHING THE HEM OF THE GARMENT

We bring to you the blessings of the masters. May you enjoy every full measure of the infinite abundance of the Eternal Heart of Love. Peace be unto each one of you, now and throughout the ages, as it has been from the beginning. Peace is man's infinite inheritance.

Long since should man have known this and enjoyed its every full measure, had it not been for the confusion of the mundane sphere. But you are coming to that place along life's path where you can say, as the humble Galilean has said, "Though I am in the world, I am not of it."

We are not going to speak about women. We shall refer to one woman. One woman who called forth from the Galilean a virtue. All mankind is possessed of the same virtue . . . love. The story I am going to relate, each one of you undoubtedly is familiar with, for at some time or other, you have read of it, in what you have learned to call the Holy Writ.

You will remember that the Galilean was traveling along the road and as was customary, as soon as he was heard of, people left their homes, their work benches and followed him. And they gathered about him to listen that they might hear of the Power of God. Immediately about the Galilean stood his twelve disciples and about the twelve disciples gathered the throng of people to listen. It is not always truly narrated in your Holy Writ as to why the twelve disciples stood immediately about the Galilean.

For one to learn they must listen and in order to listen or be able to listen, there must be order. Therefore the twelve disciples kept order. For where there is confusion, there is little understanding and that you have found to be true. In reading of the story you will remember that a certain woman whose physical body had been smitten over a period of twelve years with what the narrative refers to as an issue of blood . . . this woman beheld the throng. And so great the throng, that she was unable to see the Galilean, let alone touch him. And as she stood at the edge of the throng with the desire to behold his countenance, to come in closer contact with Him to receive a healing to her body, the desire so welled within her that at last she bent to her knees—that symbolizes *humility in thinking*. And as she bent to the ground or knelt to the ground she crawled on her hands and knees between the feet and legs of the throng and touched the hem of his garment.

What is man to understand from the press of the throng? When man has the spiritual significance of the narrative and he understands contact with God, the "press of the throng," is but symbolic of *confusion in man's thinking*.

As her desire became great that she might receive a blessing to the healing of her body, she elevated her thinking and in consciousness humbled herself and touched the hem of the garment.

What is man to understand by the "Garment" of the Galilean. The "Garment" means but one thing. The Galilean was clothed with the virtue of the Father and thus it was not necessary for the woman to touch His hand nor to look into His face . . . merely through humility, desire, earnestness, but to touch the hem of the Garment. As she touched the hem of the Garment the Galilean spoke forth in these words. He said, "Who hath touched me? For this very moment a virtue did leave me."

The disciples wholly unmindful of what was taking place said, "Master no man hath touched Thee, for the press of the crowd is too great."

The Galilean said, "Verily so, this moment one hath touched me."

Then the woman spoke and said, " 'Tis I who hath touched Thee and behold my body is healed. For twelve years had I an issue of blood and I have spent all my worldly goods and no man gave unto me comfort. But this very moment the flow of blood has stopped and my body is whole."

And the Galilean answered and said, "Go thy way good woman for in this hour thy faith hath made thee whole." Listen to the statement! "Go thy way, for in this very hour thy faith hath made thee whole." The Galilean took no credit for what took place. The woman had heard of the myriad healings throughout the length and breadth of the land. Desire for the wholeness of her body became preeminent in consciousness and undoubtedly she said "I shall find this man." Desire took her to the man. Faith . . . faith, dear hearts, hath made her whole.

Let your faith be so quickened. Let your twelve disciples keep order for you and the press of the throng shall not interfere with those who desire to touch the hem of your garment. Remember you are "Christs" incarnate. You have that virtue which the sick of body, the troubled of mind, the broken of heart, seek. Keep yourself in readiness, as you travel the highways and byways of life and you are encountered by those whose hearts are heavy, whose paths are darkened with despair; those who have known of God, but lost God, in the confusion of mortal thinking; and perchance those who never knew God. For remember dear hearts, many are the so called teachers who teach of God.

May I repeat the few familiar lines?

> "Part of the sun in the apple,
> Part of the moon in the rose,
> Part of the flaming Pleiades
> In everything that grows.
> Out of the vast comes nearness,
> For the God of Love of which man sings
> Has put a little bit of His Heaven,
> Into every living thing."

Dear hearts, a part of His Heaven . . . it is spelled in these letters L-O-V-E, Love. That is the part of Heaven in every living thing. Man may deny, man may blaspheme. Man may vilify, condemn and persecute, but with all, dear hearts, remember there is something which man loves. Every man loves something and regardless of that which man loves, be not concerned. Ever be mindful that man loves and where Love is, *nothing can be lost. Where love is there can be no hellfire and brimstone. Where love is redemption is in evidence. Where Love is restitution can always be made.*

Do not be too concerned over what a man has been, over what a woman has been. Let not a reputation even as man or woman of earth creates because of their own undoing, interfere with your recognition of the "Christ" of God.

Keep your light burning; keep your bowl well filled with the oil of Love, the wick well trimmed with kindness, and that which protects the flame from the wind, well cleansed and polished with the ointment of understanding. Let your light shine. As the Galilean of old, though you stand in the press of the throng, there shall be those who shall find you; and in humble desire, in heart's consciousness, there shall be that genuflection and they shall reach through the press of the crowd to touch the hem of your garment. You shall know it for you shall feel the release of the virtue. How shall you feel it? Well, let me put it in very crude language. It will make you feel so good inside. You will feel free. You will feel big. You will feel great *inside.* Whatever you turn your hand to do shall no longer be an effort. There will be no difficult tasks.

For a life surrendered unto the innate father, the indwelling father is that which keeps your temple clean, keeps your garment magnetized with the Christ virtue. There shall be those who cross your path and a casual handshake may perchance cause them to shudder, as it were, and to themselves they may say, "My what a feeling came from that handshake."

The more of love you use the more you shall have to use. Remember the Galilean's well never ran dry, dear heart . . . never ran dry. We are told that in His very last breath He said, "Father, Father forgive them, for they know not what they do." Was the Galilean referring to what they were doing to His body? Ah! Had our theologians but told the Truth, no indeed, THAT was of lesser import to the Galilean, for that He could endure.

What did the Galilean mean when He said, "Forgive them for they know not what they do?" He was thinking of those who persecuted him. He was thinking of those who handed him vinegar and gall to quench His thirst. He was thinking of those who drove the nails in the hands and feet. He was thinking of the one who pierced His side. He was thinking of what they were doing *to themselves* and He was asking the Father's forgiving Love, to them and for them, that even they would walk free.

Yes, dear hearts, you have had vinegar and gall offered to you to quench your thirst, you have had nails of persecution driven in your hands and your feet. You have had your side riven and you have had placed upon your brow, time without number no doubt, the crown of thorns. Learn to say, "Father, forgive them for they know not what they do." And I promise you, I promise you, you shall be found in the press of the crowd and the hem of your garment shall be touched.

They are being touched now, dear hearts. They are being touched now. Many, many have benefited by the virtue you have sent forth even unto those who have been unable to touch the hem of your garment. How has this been brought about? Well it is quite simple. *You have prayed and your prayer has been one of Faith, faith, understanding, a prayer of knowing that as you uttered your prayer it was answered . . . now.*

Your prayer did not go forth in an agonized manner and you did not send them to the far off blazing Arcadia. You ascended in consciousness and you stood before the table upon which rests the Golden Salver wherein is placed the Shew-Bread of Life. There you laid your loving, humble petition. And it became illumined with the lighted tapers in the Golden candle sticks, placed upon the table of plenty at either end of the Golden Plater.

That is fervent, effectual prayer. Goodnight.

Bless you. Bless you. Bless you.

WHAT IS THE CHRIST PRINCIPLE OF GOD

With the humbleness of the All Creative Principle in Life we greet you. You have not walked alone. Ever since you have chosen the body which you now tenant, God's presence has been watching every path. Even as His eye has been upon the sparrow, it has been upon you. From incarnation to incarnation has He followed you, for He has been with you. There is no separation in God.

Now . . . it is desired of you that you fulfill the purpose for which you truly desired, the body which you now own . . . listen carefully . . . THE GREATEST JOY IN LIFE IS SERVICE. THE GREATEST POWER IN LIFE IS LOVE. AND THE GREATEST BATTLE IN LIFE IS THE BATTLE AGAINST ONESELF.

There is a difference between riches and wealth and wealth without riches is meaningless. It is God's Perfect Idea that his children shall be well fed and well cared for. *God knows nothing of poverty,* neither does God know anything of physical discomfort. The Psalmist of old has said, "He prepareth a table before me in the presence of mine enemies." *And the greatest enemy that man of earth shall ever know is in his own thinking. The greatest poverty that man of earth shall ever know is impoverished thinking; and the greatest blessing man shall ever know is the blessing of spiritual riches.*

When man becomes Spiritually rich, earthly wealth cannot be denied him. The sun of realization is now rising about the horizon on your time. Each moment you have spent in quest of truth has not been wasted. We behold in you . . . and we greet that which we behold in you . . . the Christ of the Living God. We desire to be humble in speaking with you and we have the assurance your acceptance shall be in the greatest of humility. Why are we so assured? For this reason: Along Life's path you have expressed compassion, humility, tolerance. Would you say to me, "I fear I have not?" Do not so mention. Of your spiritual substance, you have shared.

Remember and never forget . . . the only thing that *man ever holds fast unto himself is that which he gives away* and gives freely. For the more man gives, the more he shall receive. Has not the Nazarene said, "Unto he who hath it shall be added unto, but unto he who hath not it shall therefore be taken away." That sounds rather inconsistent to God's law, does it not? But it is not! "For unto he who hath not" . . . hath not what? . . . hath not consideration, hath not tolerance, hath not compassion, hath not love.

We are not eulogizing events in your life, and you and you alone shall know the truthfulness of our statement. For remember, "As his eye has been on the sparrow, so it has been on you." You have graciously served. The greatest joy in life is service . . . never forget that. And because of your understanding of the Principle of Love, you have served with power. For the greatest power in life is Love. And you have only battled with your mortal self when you, in your thinking, said to yourself, "I wish I could do more. I have done nothing. What else is there for me to do? How, in a greater measure can I be of service to my God and my fellowman?" That has been your greatest battle.

Will one of you dear ones spell for us the word Christian? Will one of you spell the word Religion . . . now will you spell the word Form? And, in the two last words that you spelled, where do you find the word Christ that you find in the word Christian? Do you find it? It is not to be found . . . of course not. Man has created forms; man has divided God into parts, because of his desire to create what he has called and still calls denominations, creeds, forms, fallacies, phantoms, fables . . . if you please. But you can only spell the word Christianity or Christian with the word CHRIST.

And there is not one Christ . . . each one of you here present is the incarnate Christ of God and do not overlook that truth. And as you exemplify that Principle in living life's pattern daily, you are living the life of a Christian . . . if you please.

Where does the word Christ come from? It is of ancient age. What does it mean? *It means Illumination . . . Light . . .* and nothing else. And when man has learned that he is the true child of a Living God; when he understands his true sonship with the Father and Mother God, he then becomes the perfect student of truth. He then becomes the perfect mystic, because of the "CHRIST LIGHT" OF GOD.

Man cannot forsake the "Christ" regardless of how he so wills to do. Man cannot find the Christ in form, fable . . . man does not find the "Christ" in creed, ritual. Man finds the "Christ" within and *only within.*

Look not for Masters round about you until you have found the Master within . . . you are masters . . . Christ masters. Each teacher in their own time, unto their own people, were God chosen and revealed the Christ of God. Man cannot serve his fellowman without love, and man cannot love, without service . . . they are handmaidens. Trus service is born from the womb of love. Has this ever been your experience?

To lift even a thimble full of water to parched lips, that is a service of love. Who did you love in so doing, what love were you expressing? . . . Your love for your God. And God love expressing through you caused you to lift the thimble full of water. Have you ever beheld someone walking along life's path and you knew they were less fortunate than yourself . . . silently you said, "God Bless You, God Bless You . . . I trust you shall have every beneficence bestowed upon you." Was that expressing love? You could not have so expressed without love, dear hearts. The greatest joy in life is service . . . the greatest power in life is love.

> Would you know Life abundant
> Love doubled, for all you give?
> There is a means no surer
> Than helping some one to live.

And the Galilean said, "Inasmuch as ye have done this unto the least of these my brethren, ye have done it unto me." He, the man Jesus? Ah nay, unto the Christ of God, not unto the physical.

Unto whom does man render service in befriending his fellowman? Yes, I will agree with you he beholds the flesh temple before his physical eye, but unto whom is the service rendered . . . unto whom is love expressed . . . that which the physical eye does *not see,* the . . . *Innate Christ . . . of God.*

This next statement I make lovingly, but I make it that you might know. Man may forsake forms, religious dogmas, and religious creeds . . . those are man made . . . mortal conceived. And I must be careful, yet I desire to be daring that you are able to separate the mixture.

Why has man formed creeds . . . isms? Unfortunately, it is born out of greed. The *unregenerate will desires to be a leader, and it is only the regenerate will that can lead.* Mind you, you may forsake form, you may disregard creeds, you may bury the phantom in the dust of itself; but you cannot forsake the Christ. You cannot forsake yourself. Thus the humble Nazarene likewise said, "What shall it profit a man if he gain the whole world and lose himself?"

You do not read it in that manner. This is the interpretation you have, "What shall it profit a man if he gain the whole world and lose his soul?" Man cannot lose himself and man cannot lose his soul identity with the Great Oversoul of the Universe. It is impossible, hence the blessing of creation . . . rebirth. Man may deny his sonship with his God, but, before the curtain falls on the last physical scene, as it were, he shall find himself . . . his true relationship with God.

The greatest joy in life is service. The greatest power is love, and the greatest battle in life is with oneself. Battle as you may, eventually, as some have termed it across the treadmill of life, man finds himself. *The Christ light of God is principle. It is not a form created, instituted, and conceived in mortal mind. May I repeat . . . Christ of God is principle and he or she who follows the Christ principle is a Christian . . . and that which they teach is Christianity. And that is the difference between man-conceived . . . may I say falderal . . . and the true principle of life.*

Now, may I be pardoned for speaking of my earthly experience, for the reason that I could not deny the Light of Truth, as it made itself evident in consciousness, and follow along in the narrow path of Orthodox Theology. I was excommunicated if you please, from the august body of the clergy. But I have not yet been excommunicated from God. What will you follow . . . forms? What in consciousness shall you become absorbed in or with . . . fables . . . idle fancies . . . or Principle? *Principle is livable with every breath you take. For it is God principle which gives you the power to breathe . . . forget it not.* And we find you radiating the Christ Principle.

There is work to do here on this mundane sphere of Life, and we of the Council need collaborators. The vines are weighing heavy with grapes and the fields are ripening. We are in need of those who shall go forth and garner. You shall not separate the tares from the wheat, while they grow together in the field; for as you go forth to teach, to share, to express the CHRIST PRINCIPLE, the tares shall become wheat. That is the service of those whom man has learned to call Mystics, Seers, Prophets, Teachers.

There is a statement with which you are familiar, dear hearts, "Many are called but few are chosen."

And you may say, "Why are not all chosen who are called?"

Let me repeat the statement, *"Many are called, but few are chosen." Who makes the choice? . . . only the ones who are called.* We call, dear hearts, in this hour we call . . . you shall contemplate the call. It is not mandatory that you shall answer. The Christ of God shall not forsake you if you deem it unwise to answer . . . if you deem it unwise to choose. For as you reckon time, some time in another embodiment, you will harken the call and make the choice.

Why are you called? For the reason that you are now ready. Down through the ages while crossing life's sands, you have served and you have always chosen a path across which have passed those who are less fortunate than yourself. Now you are ready to launch your bark forth on the Great Sea of Life. And all the knowledge you have accumulated now ripens into wisdom. And with the wisdom, you are imbued with understanding. Yes, you are a Christ disciple. Not merely a disciple to the teachings of the man Jesus . . . and with him we find no fault, God forbid . . . but you are disciples of the IN-NATE CHRIST, the same "Christ" as dwelt in Jesus, Buddha, Zoroaster, Confucius, and myriads of other teachers too numerous to mention at the given moment . . . all Christ of the Living God.

How shall you serve? As you always have, full surrender in Love. You understand Love. Some of you have laid your bodies on a very sacred altar, the altar of motherhood. In what greater manner can Love be expressed than through devotion to bring forth a physical temple wherein dwells a soul seeking to express motherhood? Let no man of earth tell you otherwise . . . the fatherhood and motherhood of God . . . Father, the Creator, Mother, the bearer and sustainer

. . . masculine, the creator, and feminine, love. And let no man of earth confound your thinking. *That is principle . . . motherhood . . .* blessed motherhood.

In the stillness of your own soul's consciousness, dear hearts, ponder the call . . . you have been rebellious in only one manner, dear heart, you have been rebellious unto error. Truth has been your principle, and truth is your principle. You have not permitted and neither shall you permit mortal man to drag you down, as it were, into the quagmire of error. This is exemplified by the Christ of God. Ponder well. We welcome you . . . we need you . . . you are a living channel through which God expresses.

It is our infinite pleasure in visiting with you. Do not become over anxious. Contemplate well within your heart's consciousness, within your soul's consciousness. Do not say "How can I do it, when shall I do it, shall I do it?" Moreover say, if you so desire . . . moreover say, "I desire to walk in the footprints of the Masters who have preceded me." Should you determine, you will find that the yoke shall be easy and the burden shall be light, for the reason that there shall be no burden.

And in parting, I make this statement lovingly: Man of earth can harness that power, elevate it in consciousness through regeneration in thinking. Have no fear of tests in your life. Have no fear.

Bless you, bless you, bless you. Goodnight.

DISSOLVING CONFUSION WITH LOVE

Though man sees not the radiance of the sun, yet it shines . . . twilight, then the darkness of the night, wherein man seeks to rest his physical temple. Darkness of the night shall bring no fear, be the day well kept with happy thinking. Darkness is but the mantle which closes round about, to bring stillness to the soul.

What has happened? What has happened in the brightness of the sun? Has mortal man been happy? Has he been in agreement with his God? Has he radiated love? Have the duties of the day been pleasant? If so, night brings no fear. There is no fear; God reigns supreme. *All that which man beholds in consciousness he becomes a part thereof.*

The babbling brook sings its song as it runs its course upon its rocky bed. It feels not the presence of the rocks, for as the water runs its course, it says to the rocks, "You and I are one with God. If it were not for you, though the current be, I could not dash and dance along my way. You and I are one." The weary wayfarer passing by, kneels to drink and the babbling brook says, "You and I are one. Drink of me, parched lips, parched tongue. Drink of me." Footsore and worn the traveler kneels to drink. Refreshed he rises and journeys on his way.

Man is a babbling brook. His voice of merriment, that which speaks the song of God, is as the babbling brook on its course. No man of earth is perfect. The approach of perfection is the path along life's highway.

Would man attain perfection in the flesh temple? If so, then he shall think in thoughts of perfect love. His thoughts shall be in harmony with his fellowman, as the waters recognize their oneness with the rocks which form their course. God is Perfect Idea and *mortal man only reaches God consciousness when he ceases condemnation of his fellowman.*

The apple would not ripen without the sun, and how would man have the light of the moon if it were not for the sun's reflection? All nature is one. All Nature is one in God. Would man have success? Would man of earth have peace? If so, then if in no other manner, let him become a blessing in his thinking.

114

The Galilean said, "Pluck not the mote from thy brother's eye and behold not the beam in thine own." With whom does man find fault when he finds fault with his fellowman? *There is no physical perfection. There is but one perfection, the perfection of spirit.* Should man feel that he has been unjustly dealt with, let him understand it is but the frailty of flesh.

For man to find fault with his fellowman is to find fault with God. God is faultless. Man cannot find fault with God. For if he endeavors to find fault with God, he is but finding fault with himself.

What matters to man of earth . . . what matters to man of earth how his fellow brother lives? When man of earth beholds the perfect image and likeness of God he will learn to bless the likeness of God and disregard the infirmity of the flesh.

Many a master of ancient days has walked the highways and byways of life in the physical temple, clothed with tatters and rags. God is no respecter of persons. We of the Council, as we have told you, are interested only in *what man is,* not *who he is, he is spirit.*

Why do we speak to you in this manner? Dear hearts, life's path is endless and to this very moment you have met with all manner of man, and yet there are men and women to meet. You are called and as you have answered this call, you have made a choice. And you have been called for the reason that you have been crossing life's sands for eons of time. Experience brings wisdom . . . experience brings wisdom. Love is God in manifestation. We shall never hear you say, "I have a regret in my heart."

Dear ones, whatever the situation, circumstance, or condition may be, we shall ever hear you say, "I am happy that God has chosen me to say, 'Bless you, bless you, bless you.' " Ah yes, ah yes beloved, there have been storms, but you have passed through the storms.

Remember and never forget, you were guided from the destruction of the rugged, rocky coast and your ship found snug harbor because some one loved you and in some moment said, "God bless them, wherever they may be . . . God bless them."

The Apostle Paul made this statement, "Evil communications corrupt good manners." And as the Apostle Paul made that statement, truth it is. There are no evil communications in Love. When you meet with that which gives the appearance of controversy, regardless of the avenue through which it is expressed, do not become alarmed; for even he who conducts himself seemingly unjust and may not be of your opinion . . . remember he is a child of God. As the water of the brook recognized its kinship with the rock upon which it moves, so all mankind is one.

"Though I have all faith," said the Apostle Paul, "that I may remove mountains, and have not Love, what doth it profit me? And now abideth Faith, Hope, Love, these three, but the greatest of these is Love."

The lowly Galilean said, "If thou be smitten upon one cheek, turn ye the other." He spoke but of tolerance. Of what was he mindful? That all mankind are of the one kinship, the image and likeness of God. Would you be released from adversity? Continue to Bless, and whatever uncomfortable circumstance you may have encountered, continuing to bless removes all adversity.

We are endeavoring to lead you in the Light of God. Night shall not frighten you. There shall be no night time of doubt. There shall be no night time of confusion. ALL CONFUSION MELTS INTO ITS NOTHINGNESS IN THE PRESENCE OF LOVE. Remember, God is Love and regardless of man's physical actions, all are of the one spirit, the Image and Likeness of God.

Continuing to Bless, the one whom you bless becomes receptive to your blessing and the frailties of the flesh are overcome. I behold you God's Image and Likeness. The rocks and the water are of the same Creator.

We speak in this manner at this moment, lest in that hour which you have learned to call the future, you may become prone to accept discouragement. NEVER BE DISCOURAGED. Man cannot be discouraged, man cannot be fearful, man cannot falter, and man shall never fall, when he fully realizes that God is his infinite supply. Every need is met through Love, and the greatest need for man is peace of mind. God is peace. How can you fail in your endeavor when you Love? Love knows no failure. "It vaunteth not itself. It is not puffed up and doth not behave itself unseemingly."

Now, dear hearts, as you travel along Life's Path, you shall continue to contact all manner of man. Remember the word *forgive.* How is it to be understood? Very simple. Give up the old for the new . . . *Give For* . . . thus you forgive. And in so doing you shall never experience disappointment.

The Galilean likewise said, "Do unto your fellowman as you would that your fellowman would do unto you." And if, in expecting a kindness from your fellowman, there is given the appearance of unkindness, continue to express in love. For that which you seek comes forth from but its own womb.

In a previous visit some mention has been made of the measuring rod. It is true. Should discouragement seemingly present itself, pause long enough to say, "What does God think of this . . . what does God think of this?"

And the answer shall come to you, "My child, I am no part of error. I am present, error is nonexistent. It shall only become existent as you accept it. I am your Father. We are one."

Peace is the wellspring of Life. Its waters never cease to flow. Drink of the waters of peace. "Blessed are the Peacemakers. I am for Peace," said the teacher, "I AM . . . I AM."

You, dear ones, are joined together to bring peace to man of earth and as you have been previously informed, man shares that which he possesses and you possess Peace. Therefore, you shall share it. Truly each one of you have grown as you have crossed life's sands. Wisdom you have gathered, therefore be merciful then as God is merciful with the unwise. For they too, as they continue their travel across life's sands, shall become wise. And they shall gather wisdom because your path has crossed with theirs.

Wisdom knows no condemnation. Let me again quote the Apostle Paul, "Evil communications corrupt good manners . . . As a man thinketh in his heart, so is he." When that which has become worn threadbare in your consciousness, it is of no longer service to you, dear hearts. Cast it out . . . cast it out. Give up the old for the new.

Be not as Lot's wife, do not take one little peek, *for a peek to the worn out past retards man's onward progress.* "Let the words of my lips and the meditations of my heart ever be acceptable in Thy sight O God; my rock and my salvation."

If you had a wound on your body and you were seeking to heal it, would you keep poking at it to see if it were healing? It would but aggravate it, would it not? Therefore, "Unto Caesar that which is Caesar's, and unto God that which is God's." It is love that brings us to you. Each step you take is but another step in the path of progress wherein you shall be able to share *the great comforts of Life . . . peace unto your fellowman.*

Yes, you shall gather sweet grapes for the wine press. And to each one of you here present, this we grant . . . Peace. "There is a way which seemeth right unto a man, but the end thereof is death." The Spirit never suffers annihilation. Do not misunderstand the statement I am about to make; but if, when the human body lies cold and dormant, if that were the sum total of life's span, how well it would be for many who have become crushed with their wearisome burden, not knowing that the yoke upon their shoulders and the burden they carried was but the reflection of previous desire.

Your God is merciful, without condemnation . . . all love, dear hearts. And in the great supreme idea, there are many gates through which man passes. As he discards one flesh form he but chooses another, because of the manner in which he lived in desire consciousness, while a tenant in the body he discarded. All of this wisdom you have. It is not a decree of God that man should so pass from rebirth to rebirth. *He or she who lives in ignorance of that fact is the one who experiences such.*

He who has gleaned the wisdom of the liberation through rebirth is the wise child of God. And *he has gathered that wisdom for the reason that somewhere along the path he has met one or many who have shared that truth with him and have brought the Truth into the present incarnation.* You, dear ones, are way-showers, torchbearers. You have walked through dark valleys and because you have walked through dark valleys with your torch of Light lifted high, those who follow you walk not in darkness.

We love you. We have endeavored to leave with you a few thoughts of encouragement. You should have never been called if you had not earned this right to serve. We Bless you. Peace shall be your goodly portion. "For out of the vast comes nearness, and the God of Love of which you sing, has put a little bit of His Heaven into every living thing."

Love life . . . love life, dear hearts . . . love it. It is not bitter. And because you love life you shall sweeten the cup of others.

Goodnight, Bless you.

JUDGE NOT—GOD IS NO RESPECTER OF PERSONS

We thank you for this opportunity to visit with you. We trust we shall be ever able to leave with you words of comfort, encouragement, and in some wise help to brighten roads upon which you are traveling, both physically and spiritually.

There is peace for man. *It is within the keeping of each man of earth to live in peace. But man shall learn that it is he and he alone who shall establish peace.* The Psalmist of old said, "Though a thousand shall fall at thy right hand, and a thousand at thy left hand, it shall not come night unto thy dwelling." When man becomes spiritually illumined he understands that every need shall be supplied according to the riches of infinite abundance. Let man seek only that which is honorable to himself as he would expect due honor from his fellowman.

It is quite easy for man to make what man has learned to call mistakes when his desire is but for physical achievements. And as in one of our earlier lessons with you, dear ones, we used the statement of old, "It is an unwise child who becomes burned by the same fire the second time."

We have likewise mentioned that each experience along life's path is a lesson, and *if man will accept each experience as a lesson, he shall not continue to make mistakes.* When man is about to venture into that which is physically important to him, let him do as the Galilean admonished to do when He said, "Come, let us reason together."

As we have likewise previously mentioned, man has no mind . . . *there is but one mind . . . Godmind.* Therefore let man reason in this wise, "What does Godmind desire for me to do?"

The Psalmist of old likewise said, "Teach me thy way O Lord, and lead me in a plain path . . . plain path," said the Psalmist, "Because of mine enemies." Wants . . . physical desires . . . born out of physical emotions . . . become enemies.

We are not endeavoring to leave with you the thought that you shall become in the least wise negative. But in walking along the highways and byways of life, meeting with those who are less fortu-

119

nate than yourself in your present estate of life . . . and this is not negative, dear hearts . . . have you ever stopped to reason, have you asked yourself the question, "What has happened to that child of God that they are living in poverty, with a worn, torn, emaciated, physical body?" Have you ever asked yourself that question?

There is but one tangible security in life and that is spiritual. All else can rust, decay and become corrupted by the moth of emotionalism. Stop . . . Look . . . Listen . . . and remember the words of the Galilean when he did say "Come, let us reason together." And the great reasoning, the greatest reasoning of all reasoning takes place between the mortal and the spiritual.

Stop and ask, "What does God desire me to do?" Then look. . . . "In what direction does God desire for me to move?" then listen. . . .

And that which man has called the still small voice shall speak and say to you, "Child of God, this which you desire, is it want or need . . . is it want or need?"

When man can dedicate his life wholly and solely to God, and with every act say, "This is wholesome. I can dedicate this to God's service, God shall be pleased with this act. God shall be pleased that I committed this deed unto him."

Will you pardon me for a moment, please if I refer to personal experiences I had when living in a flesh body? Quite frequently, in calling upon parishioners and rather unexpectedly, quite often there would be a hurry and a scurry before my summons at the door was answered. And in all the hurry and scurry, I would behold evidences of what was taking place when I sounded my alarm at the door. But they did not want their pastor to find them so engaged.

There is an infinite pastor . . . God the Creator . . . not in a far distant clime, dear hearts, but within man's heart's consciousness. *He sees because you see. He hears because you hear.* Man of earth becomes troubled at times with that which he calls conscience, but conscience could never be, dear hearts, if it were not for consciousness. God cannot be excluded. When man of earth understands this he shall have no fear. He shall have no fear of error for the reason he shall not commit error. Your God in your consciousness is yours. God is the SILENT LISTENER to EVERY conversation . . . the UN-SEEN GUEST AT ALL TIMES.

When man or woman becomes fearful it is because they are conscious of committing error. They are conscious of their disobedience to God. Blessed is it though, that God holds no man in account. God knows no discouragement . . . God knows no contempt . . . God knows no malice . . . God knows no physical discomfort. All that I have mentioned are attributes of the mortal and they exist only but for the reason of man's disobedience in his thinking. "If thy eye be singled unto the light, how great is the light thereof, but if thy eye be singled unto the darkness, how great is the darkness thereof."

Man quite often revels in the pleasantries of life when there are no storm clouds in his sky. And when the storm clouds gather he says to himself, "Why should I be caught in this storm?"

The Nazarene gave acceptable words to man when He said, "Man liveth not by bread alone, but by every word which proceedeth forth from the mouth of God." And when in consciousness God speaks, there need be no fear, ever. Dear hearts, never become impatient.

You have heard these words I am about to speak many times, "God moves in mysterious ways his wonders to perform."

And another of earth gave men these words, "The mills of the God's grind slow and exceedingly small." The mills of the Gods . . . *false ideas . . . graven images . . . of distorted thoughts . . .* the mills of the Gods. But the God of Life moves the manner in which man gives God the opportunity.

When God seemingly moves slowly in man's affairs it is because God in consciousness, is removing the obstacles of the past . . . removing the fire so the unwise child becomes wise and does not burn itself again. When progress is seemingly retarded . . . STOP . . . and say to yourself, "God loves me. I am His child, His image and likeness. God does not decree this for me, what have I done? Where have I cluttered the path?" False idols . . . graven images . . . disobedient thoughts.

There is ONE MIND . . . GODMIND. It is the Infinite Will of God that man shall live in peace with righteous power and plenty. We quite often hear man of earth make this statement, "I will not turn a finger to help." Have you met along Life's path he or she whom society calls a derelict, a derelict of society, but fortunately there are no derelicts of God. Where was the misdemeanor committed in the consciousness of he or she whom society calls a derelict? Moth ate through and rust decayed and corrupted and he or she whom you behold as a derelict once enjoyed the fullness of God's abundance. We say to you, dear hearts, the only tangible thing in Life is SPIRIT-UAL and man is worthy of every comfort, every peace of mind, every expression of God's abundance.

May I repeat, it is not God's will that man should live in poverty . . . *it is not God's will.* But when man stops to say, "Father, this would not be in my possession if it were not for you. You gave me the intelligence, you provided the avenue through which I traveled to acquire this when my body became tired standing at life's work bench, you refreshed it in sleep Father. All I have Father, it is yours . . . You are sharing it with me Father, and I shall take very good care of it."

Dear hearts, dear hearts of God . . . with malice toward none, as the statement has been coined, so true it is, "God is no respecter of persons." Comforts . . . Peace of mind . . . Health of body have been found. Each one of you here present have been through centuries of time . . . as you reckon time . . . been under the watchful eyes of your God.

Man's God is as man thinks and live in love. Forget it not and the time is not far away, when you shall have sufficient of God's abundance, more so than in this present hour, and you shall be happy . . . you shall be happy for you shall have learned of the fullness of God's immutable law of life.

For every kindness, for every expression of Love, for every service you have rendered to your fellowman, dedicated to God, your abundance shall be multiplied. Peace of Mind? O yes! You have enjoyed peace of mind, but greater peace of mind you shall have. When you see smiling faces, more in number than you have ever beheld, sick worn bodies restored to health . . . you have given witness to a few . . . but in comparison to your experience of that which you have learned to call the future, that which you beheld is in the minority.

And when, dear hearts, and when peace shall reign universally because you have been good stewards of God and you shall . . . for you are putting life's scale in perfect balance. Man of earth physically seeks to find his equal if he can, and quite often discards meeting a master because he does not behold the individual as his equal. And that is another caravan along life's road man misses.

God is no respecter of persons and we of the Council are happy to continue to visit with you . . . mind you well . . . dear hearts, *spiritual perfection is never reached in the flesh, but with few exceptions.* We do not find our collaborators Spiritually perfect and do not expect to find them spiritually perfect but we can lead you, dear hearts, and to the hour you have nobly followed.

Now may we leave you but before we do in parting may we say be of good courage . . . rejoice . . . let each word you speak ring with the sweetness of love, and ever continue to say, even though it may be silently so, "Bless you, dear hearts, bless you, I love you . . . you are God's child come up higher." It is using ones thought in a most thrifty manner. For remember dear hearts, never forget . . . I admonish with you, *for man to receive a blessing he must become a blessing.* Even though it is silently . . . may I repeat . . . even though it is silently, say "bless you, dear heart, I love you, bless you."

Thank you for your kindness and go forth with God's Breast Plate and the sword of Love. And how shall you use the sword of Love? Well, it is simple, by separating the *untruth from truth, by separating the unreal from the real, and the darkness from the light.*

Goodnight dear hearts. Bless you.

DO NOT INTERPRET TRUTH TO SUIT YOURSELF

We thank you for according us this privilege of visiting with you. We trust we shall be able to bring you some note of encouragement, as you continue your journey along that Spiritual path which leads to the fullness of the Great White Light.

It is not a cumbersome duty in accepting God's Spiritual Truth. And as we have previously stated there are times when to all physical appearances you shall not be understood nor accepted. That which you read in the Holy Writ is ever enlightening to man of earth, as he applies himself to understand it. Man of earth is prone to make his own interpretations to suit circumstances as they arise, wherein he may be of his own mortal opinion, that he is vindicating himself of some wrong.

The Holy Writ, or the Scripture as you refer to them, is a text book of Life . . . Godman's life with God . . . And points the way to enlightenment to mortal man if he so desires to accept. Many among the mortal congregation, shall I say . . . deem it too great a responsibility, to bring about renunciation . . . as it were . . . to certain mortal or physical inclinations. That is but an appearance of error. *When man of earth seeks to interpret any truth to his own liking regardless of where the Truth is found, he is not deceiving his fellowman to the degree that he is deceiving himself.*

It is within reason that every man of earth shall know and understand his true relationship to God. And it is not necessary for man to refer or resort to printed text books. They are an aid. They are an assistance. They help to encourage man until his desire and when I say his desire, I am speaking of the Spiritual Desire, when man's spiritual desire becomes illumined and to the degree that he becomes honest with himself . . . and because of his honesty with himself, he sees his fellowman in the same light. Then having found a desire for honesty with himself, he makes certain renunciation to the mortal. As he renounces certain claims and possession to that of the mortal which has held him from beholding himself the true child of God, he supplants that which he has renounced, with the spiritual desire to seek beyond the written page in preparation to read and understand the unwritten law.

Where shall he find the unwritten law? Upon the pages of the eternal cosmos. There is no reason for man to endure the darkness of superstition, only as he so desires to remain dependent upon that which expresses darkness. As we have previously mentioned, MORTAL MAN IS A WEAKLING and beyond the weakness of mortal limitation, lives the SPIRITUAL GIANT. It is not the will of God that man should remain subject to error. And you, dear ones, shall soon have the proof that God gives expression through everything that expresses life. You are standing upon the threshold of that open door now. And I believe our statement needs no further explanation. It is for that reason that we continue to admonish with you, dear ones, to abandon every form of emotionalism and become calm and receptive to inspiration of God.

Then it shall be, and only then, that you shall be able to turn the PAGES OF THE UNWRITTEN LAW. You have them now in consciousness, if you please . . . for in consciousness spiritually so, you have never been anything else but a part of God. *Emotionalism is physical.* It is born from the womb of the five physical senses. Now remember, dear hearts, *there is only one perfection and that is divine perfection. Try as you will and let me make it more general please . . . let man of earth try as he may, try as he will, to bring about physical perfection without understanding his spiritual birthright with God, and he but becomes a part of emotional confusion.* It cannot be otherwise.

THERE IS NO CONFUSION IN GOD. Now let us try to reason with you. Since physical distress to many is a reality . . . which it is not . . . but to many it becomes a reality. When that physical distress has reached its highest ebb and causes man all manner of distress and chaos, and someone comes to such an individual and says, "I too endured that."

And the other one says, "But you are not enduring it now?"

"No" is the answer.

The next question, "Then how did you overcome it?"

"I sought and found God."

Now let us reason further. If God were confusion, how then in seeking, finding and knowing God . . . if God were confusion . . . could God overcome confusion, if God were a part of it? That is not conducive to common sense logic, is it? God is the Perfect Idea and man is His image and likeness.

If you were to discover that this dwelling were enveloped in flame or fire would you undertake to extinguish that fire by starting another fire? I dare say not. Have we not reasoned with you dear ones? Man can only help his fellowman by refusing to acknowledge confusion and distress.

You may be misunderstood by your fellowman who is not as far advanced as you may be spiritually, because you do not sympathize with his dilemma in which he finds himself. But he or she who becomes adept in applying the law of God, listens patiently to all sorrow and all woe and continues silently to declare, "I am no part of it, I see no confusion. God is Perfect Peace, I am His child, His image and likeness."

How is this to help the one who is pouring out their heart of chaos and strife? Are there two of you? . . . but physically so. But you are one spiritually. You are the image and likeness of God . . . one Spirit . . . the Spirit of God seeking to express, manifest, radiate . . . through two physical temples . . . one the "I am" consciousness of God. Therefore in silence you say, "I am peace." you are claiming your oneness with perfect spirit and you are giving no recognition to mortal . . . or call it physical if you so care . . . confusion.

Why does man become confused mortally? For only one reason, that by way of physical desire he is reaching forth for something to satisfy a mortal or physical ambition and it is much more difficult to acquire and never quite as lasting, if you please. As though in patience he would say, "I am your child, Father. All there is for me to have, you have created. I desire but to claim my rightful own in thee." That is renouncing error and declaring the fullness of the incarnate Christ of which you are.

Patience, beloved. Patience and tolerance are handmaidens. They walk down the path of life, hand in hand. They are not two separate entities, so to speak. They are one.

Now may I further reason with you please? Can you turn back the pages in your memory and find where you have made what man has learned to call mistakes? And as you find them, aha! Can you say to yourself "What decision did I make when this took place? . . . and how hasty was my decision?"

Why does man meet with what he calls unkindness at the hands of those whom he reckons as his fellowman? There is no mystery to it . . . There is no mystery to it! There is an immutable law. God's law is perfect. That is the immutable law of perfection. And there is a law which man in his mortal reasoning establishes, and mortally so, that becomes immutable and sometimes must be met.

When man pauses to think upon himself as God's image and likeness with the desire of spiritual guidance, and all that which physically confronts him . . . this shall be his discovery . . . he may become physically disappointed. But what will happen? A *new avenue will open up* and soon that which he has beheld as physical disappointment shall have vanished into its native nothingness.

There are many men and women here on the physical plane of life and, perchance, you have met with and associated with some of those of whom I am going to speak. Their physical desires for achievement in certain directions so beset them that . . . may I use the term . . . that, unthinkingly, to make that particular achievement they attracted to them certain individuals who later on, as the pattern unfolded itself, became traitors . . . heartaches . . . disappointments . . . all manner of grief. I am speaking of physical attributes, please.

And yet, when that one, through some particular channel, found God, either through the kindness of a friend, or through some other means . . . they found God, and God said, "I behold no mistake. Come, you have placed your hand in the Father's Hand Now. You had it there in the beginning, child, but you became physically ambitious and you walked in the night of folly. I tried to speak to you, child, but your ear became deafened to me. You did not hear." You are now back in the Father's house. You never left it, but in consciousness you are back in the Father's house. Listen carefully.

Do not become physically ambitious. Do not reach for that which is not within your grasp . . . reach for it spiritually, my child, and you shall find it within your grasp physically . . . and when you find it physically *it shall be untarnished. It shall be pure gold and not brass . . . it shall be a precious pearl . . . it shall be a flawless diamond.*"

That is the threshold you dear ones are standing upon. You now have confidence that there is a God. Mortal man seeks some tangible evidence. That is a mortal requisite. Let me give you happy news. It shall not be too long until you shall have a tangible evidence born from the womb of spiritual truth.

Guard well that which you now have. For remember, you have it on the inside of the sheepfold, and there is only one door to that sheepfold. No one can climb over the wall for there is a protection there. He or she who would try to enter the sheepfold by climbing over the wall, shall be pricked by their own nettles.

One by one the called and the chosen shall enter the door of the sheepfold, and as they approach that door, it shall not be physical or mortal curiosity, it shall be spiritual desire to become a spiritual part thereof.

May I take you to the prayer of the humble Galilean, when He said, "Our Father in Heaven." He did not say, "Your Father in Heaven." He did not say, "My Father in Heaven." He said, "Our Father in Heaven." Man only recognizes God as the Universal Father as he ascends in consciousness, annihilating into its native nothingness all prejudice, all tyranny, all strife.

Do not weary yourself, dear hearts, that you shall ever become a part of strife and chaos while you hold fast to the realization of your oneness in the wholeness of the eternal oversoul of life which man, down through the ages, has learned to call God.

It is only when man takes his eyes from God and becomes emotionally a part of mortal confusion, identifying himself with the physical which is unregenerated . . . by the lack of the regeneration of the spirit . . . that man sinks into the quagmire of mortal distress and limitation.

Man becomes hasty because of mortal desire. Remember an old adage. It is worthy of consideration. "Haste makes waste." It is Truth.

God is everpresent . . . never tardy . . . and KNOWS NO DESERTION. It is man who in his mortal unregenerate will separates himself from God. Goodnight. Thank you.

SOUNDING BRASS AND TINKLING SYMBOL

Let there be light. Let every thought be happy. Let every word speak of Peace. It is the unwise man who makes an idle statement. For he who thinks from the innermost depth of his being, shall speak no word which shall later betray him. First let man say to himself, "What am I? For what purpose do I meet my fellowman along life's Path?"

Man can have no lasting peace of mind when, out of idle fancy he seeks to covet that of the confidence of another, unless he, in his heart's consciousness, has learned fidelity. It is unfortunate that many who have gleaned a little knowledge, seek to become leaders, as it were. Knowledge, when guarded righteously, becomes wisdom. Wisom never becomes a Betrayer.

Woe betide unto the man whose tongue speaks as a tinkling symbol, for he betrays none other than himself. *It is not all who speak of God who are faithful to God.* It is not all who say, "I understand all mysteries." For their understanding becomes lacking, and quite *often such statements are made to mislead.* It is as the one who takes grains of sugar and pollutes them with a poison, that they may attract the fly, that is causing the fly to meet its end.

Likewise it is unfortunate that such a one cannot endure, should a phantom out of the past come forth and say, "I challenge you. You have created me and you are now trying to hide me, behind the words of a silver tongue. I claim you now. Drop your mask that your fellowman may behold you as you are." The Galilean knew when He said, "I send you forth and you shall meet many wolves in sheep's clothing."

"Test the Spirit," said the Apostle Paul, "and see that it is of God." And he but repeated the statement of another sainted one. "To he who deceives, he shall but stand at the mercy of deception. There is no other alternative along life's path."

It is written, and quite frequently mentioned, "The mills of the Gods grind slow and exceedingly small or fine." There are many who live, as man of earth would say, a life of pretense. We hear them, we see them. You dear ones, are precious in our sight, and we shall see no evil befall you. Bear you this well, we shall see no evil befall you.

Each one of you are worthy of every happiness, every peace of mind, all abundance, health of body; and sweet, righteous, honorable companionship. And we shall see it no other wise. No wolf in sheep's clothing shall lead you into a stray fold. We shall not see pretense blind you. You have been guided with a watchful eye over eons of time. Let no man of earth who speaks with a silver tongue say to you, "You are being misled." You are standing on the threshold of the door of happiness. What shall be your greatest happiness? The happiness you are bringing to others. You shall not fail. Why shall you succeed? May I tell you?

That which you are pursuing is not with the thought for an accumulation of Caesar coin. *It is he who speaks with a silver tongue, with the tongue which is made of brass, who seeks Caesar's coin.* Your interest lies in devotion. Why do you recognize devotion? May I tell you please? Each one of you within the hearing of our voice, as well as others who are not present, have traveled over a rough road, and there are yet a few spaces in the road which are not too smooth. Do not become discomforted. Over-anxiousness brings a disquieting feeling you know. Be not so, dear heart, be not so. For your knowledge has turned to wisdom and you can endure. For he who seeks in Love and accepts in Love, can surrender in Love, should surrender needs be. It is the one who has lived behind the mask who says, "I cannot endure this." But they have told others how to endure. How come their endurance failed?

Well, dear hearts, it is simple. One cannot depend upon that *which one has never possessed, can they? He who purports to possess Principle and has it not, stumbles over his own rock of deception.* You have within your grasp a priceless Jewel, the Pearl of Precious Price. Dear hearts, *you are seeking your at-one-ment with your God,* and you are seeking it zealously. Therefore, it is the Pearl, Priceless unto you.

And, should the darkened hour cross your path, you can say, "I have no fear, for I have been honest with my fellowman." That is the priceless pearl. Honesty, honor is earned, dear hearts. Man cannot buy it with Caesar's coin, that you know, honor . . . honor . . .

honor . . . It is Priceless. Test the spirit of man . . . and see that it is
godly. And when it has so proven to be, you can accept it as your
sacrament in God, and you can so do without fear.

Remember, honor is earned. It is priceless. Be at peace, dear hearts,
let nothing fret you. Take your portion of life as you have it. Cherish
it, look about you, behold those less fortunate than yourself, countless
numbers they be. It is the kind you shall help. That is the stewardship
entrusted in your care. That is the father's business you are about. Be
happy and let no man of earth deceive you by saying, "You are
walking in the dark, blindly." You are not. You are walking in the
light.

There is but one Love and that is the love of God. And no man or
woman of earth can say to another, "I love you," and make that
statement truthfully so, until that man or woman has learned the
love of God. For without knowing the Love of God, mortal love
becomes as a sounding brass and tinkling symbol. Love, yes . . .
Love, the Greatest Power man can Possess. "I Love you," The greatest benediction ever pronounced. "God Bless You, I love you," sincerely spoken from the heart, without expectation of reward, heals
the wounds of the universe, forget it not beloved.

"For Love vaunteth not itself, is not puffed up, does not behave
itself unseemingly." Remember that. *Love as the Love of God never*
becomes a destructive snare . . . and he or she who desecrates love,
brings but the timber of his own structure down upon his head. Love
. . . Love . . . Love . . . Priceless.

When man says to his fellowman, "I love you," he is saying to
God, "I love you." For remember, dear hearts, man is the image and
likeness of God, and be sure when you say. "I love you," you are
beholding the likeness of God . . . and not the coin of Caesar.

Now each one of you in your present estate are happy, for you are
now in possession of your own rightful treasures. Weigh them wisely.
Each one of you stand free in the light of God. Free . . . unshackled
. . . free. Love is freedom. What shall man barter for it? What shall
he offer in its stead? Look within, dear hearts, and there find wounds
that have been healed and say, "I am happy . . . I am happy."

Dear hearts, never extend your hand openly to receive unless you
are willing to accept that which is placed in your open hand. Look at

the coin with the wisdom of the master, and when love lays in your open hand, there is no room for Caesar's coin.

Now, dear hearts, labor together, labor together. Remember you have a priceless cargo to deliver, a priceless cargo to share. And let no man of earth say to you, "You are deceiving yourself, it cannot be. You will fail." Do not listen . . . for it is "sounding brass and tinkling symbol."

You shall rejoice and from this moment henceforth let these words be your watchword, "God directs my every action. I see with the light of God, I shall not be blinded by mortal deception. God is my light." You shall not be led down the path of another's disappointment. *Let he who has met with disappointment because of deception to his fellowman,* walk in his own disappointment. You have chosen a bright path . . . honor.

Each one of you have been chosen because you have borne well your cross, and your cross no longer crucifies you, dear hearts. You are free from the crucifixion of the flesh and no mortal mischief shall serve to be a crucifixion. We love you. Listen well, remember . . . honor always recognizes Caesar's Coin and says, "I will be no part of you. I have the Pearl of Precious Price. Be gone Caesar, I need you not."

Now we trust you shall receive the Light of this visit . . . Each one of you, Love, dear hearts, permits no evil to enter your domain. Evil becomes annihilated into its native nothingness, in the presence of Love. Be not given over to physical emotions, dear hearts. *That is Caesar's coin. Dissolve it . . . melt it . . . away with it . . . in the presence of love. Be honest . . . love endures eternally.*

It is not but from sunrise to man's sunset. It is not measured by the seconds, minutes, hours on man's time piece. It is eternal. And he who uses it idly, but by word of mouth, shall meet with its likeness ere his journey along life's path becomes complete.

Man only meets, dear hearts, that which man creates . . . MAN ONLY MEETS THAT WHICH MAN CREATES. And he who thinks in haste, speaks in haste. But he who thinks with the wisdom of God, speaks with the deliberation of honor and trust.

Goodnight, dear hearts.

FREEDOM BORN OF WISDOM

High as the mountain,
Deep as the sea,
Vast as the ocean
Our love is for thee.
As free as the lark,
In song and in flight;
With the swiftness of winged,
We bring you the Light.
Sweet as the clover
Of field vast and wide.
God's mercy is showered
Into each man's life.
Bright as the sun,
Bright as the stars;
As steadfast God's wisdom
With man not to depart.
High as the mountain,
Deep as the sea,
Vast as the ocean
God's love is for thee.

The lowly Nazarene has said, "Seek and ye shall find, knock and the door shall be opened unto thee, ask and ye shall receive." Upon what door shall man knock? Of whom shall man ask? Where shall man seek? Man's doubt is the door. It is that upon which man shall knock. Who shall answer his summons? None but the Christ within. Against whom man in his doubt, has closed the door.

What shall man ask of the imprisoned Christ? He shall ask but for the Christ to come forth. What shall man seek? Freedom, from the bondage of doubt and fear. How long has the Christ dwelled within the consciousness of man? Man is the incarnate Christ of God. And, as the Great Light sent forth its numerous illumined particles, they went forth because of the word of God, "In the beginning was the word and the word became flesh."

Desire is the word and the word continues to be Creative. God has never ceased to create. Man the incarnate Christ of God, continues on . . . the Creator. There is but the right path to pursue, for God's law is just. It is righteousness. There is *no error in God*. Man, *in mortal consciousness becomes the creator of error.*

You will remember the first words spoken in fear. The lesson is taught in allegory, you will remember. "God spoke to Adam and to Eve. Adam and Eve feared, for they became conscious of their nakedness," as the narrative relates. How shall man interpret the statement that he may understand the Truth? Was the state of nakedness then as man understands it today? You will remember, as the story further relates, that Adam and Eve endeavored to clothe their nakedness with leaves. And the part of the physical body as the narrative delineates, was the reproductive organs of the body . . . the Life Center. What is man to understand?

Life is Power. Power is Life. The narrative further relates that the serpent beguiled Eve. Shall we go back to the beginning of the lesson? Adam, let us behold the physical Adam, an inanimate form, the narrative relates. The Power which created that inanimate form, man is told breathed upon it and it became a quickened, animated being. But it was apparently rather useless, and the narrative continues to relate that the Power which created the physical structure and then breathed upon it caused the animated being to sleep. And during the period of sleep, "Eve came forth," Again, "the Word became flesh."

Woman, born from the womb of man, hence her name . . . WO-MAN. Adam became a quickened being in the Light of the day. Sleep overcame Adam, symbolizing the darkness in consciousness . . . eventide. And through the stillness of the eventide, Eve came forth.

There are two serpents, dear ones, the serpent of wisdom . . . which is the quickening power of God! And the serpent of that which man has learned to recognize as evil. Evil is nonexistent in God. When did Adam and Eve, as the narrative relates, find themselves naked? Man was told it was at the time that the serpent beguiled Eve, and told Eve that the fruit of the tree was to be eaten of. The Fruit of what tree? The fruit of the tree of knowledge, does the narrative relate? But it does not relate the fruit of the *tree of wisdom, mortal conception deceives.* That is the serpent which beguiles. *Knowledge does not reveal the fullness of life . . . Wisdom does.* Had Adam and Eve partaken of the Fruit of the Tree of Wisdom, they should not have beheld their nakedness. They were naked, dear hearts, of the true revealing of God.

The life centers had not become quickened and to this day man lives in a state of superstition and doubt. Your men of science have a manner in which they explain the origin of Life. *The reproductive organs of the body are helpless to function without the Light of the Serpent of Wisdom.* Where lives the Serpent of Wisdom? *In the heart's consciousness of man.* You will read in your Holy Writ that "In peace the child shall play at the hole of the asp, and the lamb shall eat straw with the lion." The lion, to man has always been accepted as the King of the forest and the lamb as the symbol of Peace. The asp is the serpent of deception, the *Child* the *symbol of innocence.*

Know no fear, no doubt, for remember the words of the humble Galilean when he said, "Suffer the children to come unto me and forbid them not, for of such is the Kingdom of Heaven." Suffer? How shall man suffer, how shall man understand the words of the Galilean? Suffer . . . it is but tolerance, patience, faith, courage, spiritual endurance. It is not chastisement. Mortal discipline as man understands mortal discipline is to encourage through patience.

Man of earth has coined the statement, which reads in this manner, "Spare the rod and spoil the child." But the Psalmist says, "Thy rod and thy staff they comfort me." How shall man spoil the child if he spare the rod? What meant the Psalmist when he said, "Thy rod and thy staff they comfort me." The Psalmist acknowledged the Love and the Protection of the Father. He did not acknowledge the rod and the staff as chastisement. For the shepherd used the rod and the staff in Love.

Man shall use the Rod of Love, he shall use the rod of love to guide the child. He shall use it in pointing the way to God and thus the child shall grow in Peace and Love. And as the child becomes man he shall not know the ferocious lion. For the Lion shall be swallowed up in Love. For there shall be no fear and neither shall the child grow in fear of the asp.

Thus the lamb, the child, the man shall eat straw with the lion. Thus the lamb, the child shall play at the hole or the nesting place of the asp, and in consciousness have no fear. The child shall never behold its nakedness or ignorance. The child, the lamb . . . the Lamb of God, which taketh away the sin of the world and in Freemasonry . . . if you please . . . the Apron, the lambskin covers the secret parts . . . as man refers to them . . . the reproductive organs which are governed by the serpent of wisdom, which has its abiding place with the lamb, in the throne seat of the living God, the incarnate Christ.

The lambskin . . . not leaves . . . the lamb which taketh away the sin of the world, and there can be no world without man. And man cannot be without God. For man continues to create and let us listen once again to the words of the lowly Galilean when He said, "Man liveth not by bread alone, but by every word which proceedeth forth from the mouth of God." There is a Tree of Knowledge, there is a Tree of Wisdom. Knowledge is but intellect. It is that part of man that must as Adam did, rest in the quiescence that Eve might come forth and there no longer be darkness. Then man shall eat at the command of the serpent of Wisdom from the TREE OF LIFE. And creation shall no longer be a mystery. Even men of science shall know that life is not born. It is but the physical body that is born. Life is the word and the word is desire and desire chooses the physical body. Life is birthless, ageless, deathless . . . and the body knows no end.

There is no annihilation to Spirit and no annihilation to the flesh. For the flesh will return to the substance from which it came, but to be used again through the law of nature, to provide another physical vehicle to carry along life's path, the soul who so desires to return.

I leave you, Bless you. Goodnight.

PALACE OF THE KING

In the presence of the masters, in the Palace of the King,
In the temple of the mighty, the Angelic Host doth sing,
Hear the music sweet and softly, it is the music of the spheres,
In the presence of the mighty, in the Palace of the King.
Scent the sweetness of the flowers, as they grow along the way,
You have spread their seed, behold, the bloom they now bring,
The radiance of your Love thoughts; seeds sown in the hearts of man,
Listen, to the fledgling grown, as they sing upon the wings,
In the presence of the mighty, in the Palace of the King.
Hear the music of good tidings, hear the message that it brings,
Peace of Mind, health of body, happiness;
In the presence of the mighty, from the Palace of the King.

Please accept our benediction of Love. Nestle it closely in your hearts, dear ones. Remember, all is well, learn to say, "I live with God. All power is given to me, in Heaven and in earth." Never forget . . . speak the words of Life.

That which you endeavor to do physically so, remember, God is your partner, God is your helper. Never attempt to lift your hand without the full realization that you are doing it with the Power of God. That is Truth. It is not fanaticism, it is truth. Every part and particle of the physical temple lives because of God. God continues to create! Man is co-creator with God. Live in the perfect realization that God's abiding place is the physical temple. Remember the words . . . "As a man thinketh so is he."

I am God's child . . . I live in the Palace of the King. God is King. I hear the music of the spheres with God's ears . . . God is Life . . . I behold the beauty of Life with the perfect sight of God. God's path is the plain path. I walk in the steps of God. My feet take me into the paths of righteousness. Once I spake as a child, I thought as a child, now, I have laid aside all childish things. I am God's man, I am God's woman. Once I saw through a glass darkly. Now I see . . . I behold face to face, I behold God in all there is. I am free. God holds me not in account. God is forgiving Love, I am forgiving Love. I live with the King, in the palace of the King. I walk and I talk with the King . . . I walk and talk with the King.

"Knock and the door shall be opened unto you, seek and ye shall find, ask and it shall be given unto thee." Dear hearts, God is no disappointment. Wait not as you listen to the seconds, minutes and hours. Measure not God's time by physical measurement. Learn to say, "Now is the accepted time. I have knocked, I seek, I ask, I doubt not, I live life with the living Christ. There is no bondage in God."

Fret not your hearts, walk steadfastly and learn to say, "All that which I do, I do with the Power of God, I live with the King, I listen to but the sweet harmonious strain of the music of the spheres, I behold but the beauty of the wonders of God, I live in the peace of God."

Have you ever 'ascended a mountain, physically so? Well, in mountain climbing there is a guide, who knows every step of the way and in olden times about the middle of the body, he fastened a rope and on either hand he held a spiked stave, and those who followed, were fastened to the same rope, and they too held in either hand, spiked staves. There is a mountain, there is a guide, there is a rope. You have found that guide. You have the staves. You are fastened to the rope. Know it well, now there is no longer a reason for you to slip back. Fast to the guide, claim it, claim it.

Speak with the mouth of God and let no word of man betray. God has created beauty for you to behold. There is no darkness in God's eyes. You are all fastened to the same rope about the middle of the same guide, and some of you have proven the trustworthiness of that rope. You shall all labor together and see the wonders of God manifest.

There is Peace, there is Power. God lives. You dear ones rejoice in that which you are called upon to do. Be merry, happy, sing, rejoice. Let your hearts overflow and as you rejoice learn to say, "God, I thank you, I can serve you."

Your bodies, the temple of the living God, the Palace of the King, shall wax strong, the marrow of its bone shall become rich. There shall be no weariness. Rejoice and be exceedingly glad for great is man's reward in Heaven. Heaven is within. It is the throne seat of the Palace of the King. Each one of you claim that power now. It IS here . . . claim it, dear hearts. Claim it . . . Claim it . . . ACCEPT, RECEIVE, APPROPRIATE . . . Accept, Receive, Appropriate.

Bless each one of you.

THANK GOD AND TRUST GOD

In the name and presence of the Most High, we greet you. Behold all things become new and unto he who forsakes the old, the new is new indeed. For that which has been in the beginning, has never become old. God's perfect idea is always new.

The Galilean said, "There is nothing hidden, but what shall be revealed and nothing covered but what shall be uncovered." Man's quest for health of body, peace of mind, and the establishment of divine order in all that he seeks to do, bringing such into manifestation, is but revealing and uncovering that which has always been. That which has been covered and unrevealed to man, because of his lack of desire to possess it. UNTIL he comes to the cross roads of chaos and finds no physical solution to the chaotic condition in which he finds himself. Thus man turns to God.

Well it is that he does. How does man solve that which he accepts and recognizes as chaos or trouble. It is simple. *God is the perfect idea and in God and Godmind there is no chaos, no confusion, no trouble.* Thus, as man turns to God, he finds that which has always been, is and shall always be perfect. He is uncovering that which has been hidden to him. Thus the Hidden becomes revealed.

There is no failure in God. As man turns to God, let him do it with patience. May we repeat a statement which we have previously made on several of our visits? Acceptance is to receive, and that which man receives he appropriates. He appropriates it in POWER OF THINKING. Man cannot pray with the right hand extended, and then with the left hand reach in to the right hand to see how the prayer is coming forth. *Man prays in confidence, in trust, in faith. Faith not just believing, but faith knowing. That is positive, affirmative Prayer. He does not listen to negative statements, as offered by those who are but schooled in the material or the physical. Their knowing is limited but to physical experiences, which has come to their attention by those who do not have founded faith.*

When man moves to God in prayer, he is not moved by negative statements of mortal mind. If you, dear ones, are seeking to purchase some item or article you would accept only that which you were in quest of. You would not purchase that which would be inferior to that which you seek. When man seeks of God, he is seeking for that which is bonafide of true worth and value.

When he listens to negative statements sent forth from those who think in terms of limitation, for the reason that they are no better schooled . . . man is examining the merchandise of Life. And when he says, "I will accept nothing inferior to that which I seek," he holds firm to God.

God has never failed man . . . man becomes impatient. Godmind is wise and never withholds from man that which is good and proper for man to possess. God is not the dealer in inferior merchandise. God's treasures are Priceless. Therefore let man have faith. God knows no time as man reckons time. Beloved, God does not test nor prove man; therefore man shall not test nor prove God. God is Faithful. Therefore man shall be faithful to God. God does not bargain with man. Therefore man shall not bargain with God.

Each one of you dear souls here present are worthy of every good and righteous gift. ALL mankind is so worthy. But you, dear ones, seek to serve God while others who are worthy, are quite often unaware that God IS. Therefore you are indeed worthy. Trust God . . . trust God.

Each one of you have in your possession negotiable drafts on the Bank of God and as you desire to cash those drafts, God accepts them and grants to you all that which the draft demands . . . trust God. Where is God? God as you know, is found in everything that expresses Life. God seeks to manifest through all that which expresses Life. Therefore, unto he or she who is limited in their understanding of God, yet called in some manner of service to their fellowman, be it your lot to encounter them, what shall you do? You shall bless them and behold that individual as yourself, the image and likeness of God. Should you be aware of the fact that they are limited in their understanding of God, how do you meet them? In this wise, as the Nazarene stood at the tomb of Lazarus He said, "Father I thank you." Why did he thank the Father? For the reason He beheld Life and not death.

The Nazarene knew that there was no death, no infirmity. Man's lack of understanding of God is but because of his lack of desire to

know God. Therefore, as you meet such an individual, you are standing before the tomb of Lazarus and you say, "Father I thank you,
Lazarus Lives."

You are calling forth the Christ from within the tomb before
which you stand. You are quickening that power of the Living Christ
within the flesh-tomb before which you stand. This Truth you can use
all along Life's Path. Therefore, you are bringing into manifestation
the statement that is written, "God's eyes are too pure to behold
iniquity."

Do not limit your pleas to God with thoughts of doubt. Whatever
your plea may be, remember, dear hearts, you are seeking light,
wisdom, understanding . . . give thanks for it . ... before you have
ever uttered your plea. And after you have given utterance to your
plea continue to thank God that your plea has been heard and
Lazarus lives.

Doubt shall then become annihilated into its native nothingness.
You shall then be bringing into manifestation the statement of
Power uttered by the Nazarene when he said, "And 'I' if 'I' be lifted
up, shall draw all mankind unto me."—Meaning the "I" of God.

Likewise the statement, "Seek, ye shall find, knock and the door
shall be opened unto you." Likewise, "There is nothing hidden but
what shall be revealed; there is nothing covered but what shall be
uncovered."

The humble Galilean has said and continues to speak, "By your
Faith are ye made whole." Man asks for health of body. He asks for
health at the moment when he is enduring or experiencing mental
despair, and then when circumstances or conditions arise for man to
prove his faith he is prone to say, "I am afraid I can not do it."

Acceptance . . . what is man accepting? Is he accepting the gift
for which he has cried or is he accepting the limitation of his own
mortal thinking? *Bless every circumstance, every condition, as it
arises and say, "With the Power of God I am quickened and I can do
it now."*

Where you seek the services of your fellowman, whether it be for
health of body or peace of mind; bless the one through whom you
seek aid and assistance. Bless them in this wise, "You are God's child,
we are one. All that which you have knowledge to do, I bless and

have no fear." *Remember, dear hearts the fervent effectual prayer of life is giving thanks.*

"Father I thank you now . . . now, Almighty One, YOU are sustaining me . . . Now I walk with power . . . I speak with power . . . I see power manifest everywhere I look." Are you deceiving yourself? No indeed. Though the Light be ever so dim, it is Light. Though the power gives the appearance of being feeble, it is power.

"For unto he who hath, it shall be added unto." Fear begats fear, Truth begats Truth, Life begats Life . . . and it can be in no other wise. We are rejoicing!

Each physical body is a laboratory. Each cell, fiber, tissue and muscle responds to Truth. THEY WILL ACCEPT DOUBT . . . THEY WILL ACCEPT POWER. Under the roof of this sanctum is another laboratory and therein you are working with nature. God created elements. They respond to Love. Let us return to the physical temple. Each cell, each fiber, muscle, tissue; each particle of the physical body is nature's creation . . . Elements of Nature if you please. Assembled by the supreme architect of the universe in the womb of woman; first conceived in the thought of man, known as desire . . . the meeting of the seed of life. And as the elements which you are working with in the laboratory under the roof of this sanctum, as nature created them, through Nature's own desire to create, so the seed thought of creation finds itself in the brain of man.

It is put into action . . . a law is established, the seed seeks fertile soil and grows and waiting for the physical temple which that growth shall produce is a SOUL DESIROUS OF RETURNING to the earth plane TO FINISH the UNFINISHED PATTERN OF LIFE.

Dear hearts, you, each one of you, have work to do. You shall do it. Do not become too concerned with the ticking out of the minutes on your physical clock. You shall accomplish.

And the Lord of Host's said, "Let there be Light." And God separated the darkness from the Light and the Light became the Glory of God. And it dispelled all darkness. There can be no darkness where the Light shines.

Let therefore, the Light of God shine in your hearts, in your soul's consciousness. For the Son of God has said, "As a man thinketh in his heart, so is he." The heart of man is but the Mind of God. Man is the image and likeness of God . . . perfect in being. Therefore, let man be ever conscious of his Spiritual creation in God.

When the Nazarene said, "I am the Way, the Truth and the Light," He was not speaking of the mortal. He was speaking of his birthright in God. Let man not be of a mortal opinion, that he is in mortal thinking the ruler and the conqueror of circumstances or situations. But moreover, let him be ever mindful that he, *the 'I am' principle of God, incarnate in the flesh, is a conqueror, the victor.* It is for that reason that the Nazarene said, "It is not 'I,' (meaning the mortal), who doeth the works, but the Father which dwelleth in me." All of error shall become resigned to its native nothingness, as man declares his oneness with God and accepts the fullness thereof.

Darkness is but of the mortal; it is created by negative thinking. It is that which clutters and obstructs the path of man. God is ever present. *God desires to be recognized, even though the man moves in a state of confusion, created by his own mortal unregenerated thinking.* Therefore, it behooves man when he says, "I shall do this or I shall do that," to *recognize but the One Presence,* the I AM of God. He can therefore, without fear say, "I shall do this, I shall do that. I can do this, I can do that."

Life holds no mystery to man. How shall man overcome that which he calls mystery? Let him momentarily take an inventory of all that which he has recognized as pain, suffering, limitation, want, lack, unhappiness, inharmony; and ask himself this question. "I have walked mortally so, in my own light, this has not profited me. I shall forsake the desire to conquer by the frailty of mortal reasoning.

Through all this which I have endured, I yet live and I but live by the Power of God. God is good and all that which I have endured as pain, suffering woe and tribulation, God has granted me the breath of Life . . . I live, and even though there has been tribulation, there have been hours of joy and happiness. I shall recognize joy and happiness in the midst of tribulation, as God's benediction of Love. And as I have experienced Joy in the midst of tribulation, I shall increase it by giving full recognition to God who has granted me joy, even though through my disobedience, I have established tribulation."

How well the Psalmist of old knew, when he had become weary with trial and tribulation, he said, "I shall look unto the hills from whence cometh my help. My help cometh from the Lord God, who hath created the Heavens and the earth." Where did the Psalmist look, where were the hills unto which the Psalmist looked? . . . WITHIN . . . TO THAT HEIGHT IN CONSCIOUSNESS WHERE GOD HAS EVER REMAINED, EVEN FROM THE BEGINNING.

Each day as man recognizes the newness of the day, it is but new to him in consciousness. But it is the eternal day of creation. As the sun rises beyond the horizon of your eastern sky, as you call it, light dispels the darkness of the night. And as the sun travels high in the heavens, as you recognize it, and as it shines round about you this very moment, man can be in mortal darkness. There is a sun in consciousness. There is the S-O-N of God of which you are. And there is the S-U-N of the S-O-N'S Love . . . claim IT. He who has lived in tribulation, trial and sorrow, is unwise that he so continues and forsakes it not. For he who has had but one moment of happiness, if it be but one moment, it shall suffice him to know that the S-U-N- of the S-O-N shines and dispels all darkness, if but for a moment. If happiness can be man's for a moment, it can be man's forever. For the humble Galilean has likewise said, "Is not a thousand years likened unto a day, and a day unto a thousand years?"

Let us reason for a moment in the mortal manner, how many seconds are there to a moment, how many minutes to an hour, how many hours in a day, how many days in your week and how many weeks in your year? Listen to reason, beloved, if then, in the small fraction of your earthly time you call a minute, you can smile and be happy, if can become ETERNAL. Listen to the words of the Galilean, "Is not a thousand years likened unto a day and a day unto a thousand years?" What will man make of his experience as he journeys along life's path? What shall he do with it? What has sorrow ever brought to a man but sorrow? What has joy brought to man but joy?

From whence comes laughter and joy but from the womb of Peace? Where is the womb of Peace, dear hearts? It is in man's thinking. How long shall man continue to live in thinking strife? Listen to the words of the lowly Nazarene when he said, "Render unto Caesar that which is Caesar's and unto God that which is God's." *Strife is bought with Caesar's coin.* PEACE OF MIND IS PURCHASED WITH GOD'S GOLD OF LOVE. God's Gold of Love is NOT COUNTERFEIT. It is acceptable by all who will share it. It is possessed by all who shall recognize their possession of it. Do not feel that it is God's will that man shall be unhappy, for it is *Not* God's will. Happiness is the priceless treasure of God. When there is seeming conflict along life's path, it is you, the spiritual you, who is crying for liberty.

Have you ever had the experience, physically so, of climbing a steep incline? It necessitated a little effort, did it not? But you desired to reach the summit of that incline. What did you do? How did you speak mentally? You said, "I am going to reach the summit of that incline." And in your thinking you created the Power of thought. Your thought became Powerful and your one objective in your thinking was to reach the summit . . . the height. And as you thought POWER every cell in your physical body responded. Strength came to your physical body and you reached the summit and then rested and renewed the power.

Man grows out of that which man commonly calls mistakes. *Do not look for mistakes,* dear hearts. Whatever physical evidence says to you, "There has been a mistake made," your answer shall be, "I shall look unto the hills from whence cometh my help." Look unto the height in consciousness. Look about you for some avenue through which to express a kindly act, a kindly deed; to speak a cheerful word to someone who is less fortunate than yourself. For remember, dear hearts, and never forget . . . there is always one walking along life's path who is enduring a greater misfortune than yourself. Each time man reaches forth his hand, he is not only helping the one unto whom he reaches but he is reaching forth to help himself.

How did the Nazarene express it, but in this wise, "And 'I' if 'I' be lifted up, 'I' shall draw all mankind unto me." *Man . . . the Godman . . . unseen to the physical eye, is the Christ of God incarnate. As you reach forth to bless, you receive a blessing. It cannot be otherwise.*

Therefore the Nazarene said, "Become not weary in well doing." Let there be a smile in your voice . . . no condemnation of another. And as you go forth seeking that which is rightfully yours, before you venture forth, bless your physical body. Bless every faculty you possess . . . And how shall you do it? In this wise, you shall say, "I am God's child, created in His image and likeness. I have dominion over this body. I am in spirit a part of all that which expresses life. I Bless all mankind with the same Power of Life as God has blessed me. I go forth to meet and to accept my good, my good awaits me, for my good is God's creation. As I am created in the image and likeness of God, my good awaits me and all this good God has created and sustains." This is *full surrender to God . . . full surrender in Love.* This is placing your all upon your altar of devotion to God which you have created in consciousness.

Man speaks of conscience. How does man create in consciousness? There is a LAW OF RETRIBUTION . . . WHO EXACTS THAT LAW OF RETRIBUTION? It is not of God. Man creates his own retribution by the manner in which lives in his thinking. But it is not necessary that man live with retribution. The appearance of retribution is saying this, "There is no road left behind you, do not step back child, for if you do, you shall fall into the abyss of error."

The appearance of retribution likewise says, "Forward in the power of God. Claim your birthright of Love. Live in the fullness of God's light. God's Light is Life. In God's Light and Life there is no darkness. What care you of what man says of you? Shall you accept man's disqualification and become a part of it? NEVER . . . for remember and never forget . . . GOD DOES NOT CONDEMN NOR DISQUALIFY HIS CREATION. That is but a mortal attribute, purchased with the coin of Caesar. It is a liar, it is a betrayer, a deceiver, a mocker of God. Have nothing to do with it. Hand it back to Caesar and foget it."

May I leave these familiar words with you.

> There is part of the sun in the apple,
> Part of the moon in the rose,
> Part of the flaming Pleiades
> In everything that grows.
> Out of the vast comes nearness,
> For the God of Love of which man sings
> Has put a little bit of His heaven
> Into every living thing.

Your fellowman is a part of you. There is a little bit of Heaven in him you know. And though he may speak but of mortal thinking, and speak in terms of disqualification, accept it not. See beyond that and what are you to look for? You are to look for that part of the sun, which is in the apple. Nothing shall upset you. You shall live in Peace. You shall live with that joy which is your birthright in God.

And God said, "Let there be Light." WHERE SHALL THE TRUE LIGHT DAWN? IN CONSCIOUSNESS. The beauty of the sunshine, the beauty of the rose, the happy voice of the babbling brook, shall mean nothing to mankind unless he beholds it in consciousness. Learn to speak with a smile in your voice, dear hearts as the rippling waters sing their song of life to the weary footworn wayfarer who needs to drink from the coolness of the babbling brook.

This is your day . . . this is your day of beginning again. All the good you have found in that which you have learned to call yesterday was established long before yesterday became yesterday to you . . . all the good you shall find in that which you call today and tomorrow, was established long before today becomes today to you and tomorrow shall become tomorrow to you.

For remember, there is but ONE DAY. So live today that when, in your thinking, it becomes yesterday, there shall be no seasons for regret . . . conscience . . . So live today that when tomorrow becomes today, it shall reflect but the beauty of that which you have lived today and there shall be no regret . . . conscience.

Live, dear hearts, live. There is Light in life for Light is of God and all that which is of God is Light. THERE IS NO DARKNESS IN GOD. For God is Spirit . . . you are Spirit. And there is no darkness in Spirit. Live in the full measure of God's Light and Life . . . God's Light and Life.

Bless you, Bless you, Bless you.

CALLING A CHOSEN ONE

Greetings:

We are indeed grateful to you dear ones. We thank you. To the dear one who has crossed the threshold of your sanctum, our sanctum, we greet you. This is a blessed privilege. We are indeed grateful for the opportunity of this visit with you dear ones. Life is full. It is filled with sweetness. It is filled with Love. God's beauty is expressed wherever man of earth so desires to seek for it. It shall not be difficult for man to behold beauty, when he beholds the beauty of God within his own consciousness . . . Beauty is everywhere to he or she who would behold it. When God reigns supreme in the consciousness of man, the tiniest blade of grass speaks of God's beauty.

My dear one, we are now speaking to you, daughter of God, who has paid your visit to this sanctum. We visit with you quite frequently in your sanctum, and not only at the specific hour that you set aside for Prayer and Meditation, but as you are engaged in the various duties of the day. We are mindful, as busy as your hands may be, crowded as your thinking may be, with duties of your own, in serving those near and dear to you . . . we are mindful that when one calls upon you for a word of comfort, your hands are never too busy to extend comfort. And you find words of Peace and Love to express.

You have traveled across life's sands over eons of time. Your quest to reach your God holds no mystery. It has been your desire and it IS your desire that man shall Live in Peace. It has been your desire, it is your desire, that you shall speak truth and truth alone. You have been very close to that which man calls the Invisible Brotherhood. Would you, here upon this mundane plane of life, walk the path with them, hand in hand?

Would you experience the inner revelation of the greatness of life? We impose no task. Love knows no task. It is because of the manner in which you have walked with your fellowman that we desire that you have a conscious knowledge of your oneness with the Unseen Ambassadors of God.

Ever since man has been . . . THE ANCIENT MYSTICAL WHITE BROTHERHOOD AFTER THE ORDER OF MELCHI-

150

ZEDEK HAS BEEN . . . Unto each man of earth is allotted a portion of Life's pattern, in each physical incarnation. You have followed your pattern well. It is our desire that you become in conscious recognition, another one of our Ambassadors here, on this, your physical plane of life. Would you so desire to accept, my dear ones? We shall impose no duty greater than that you have already assumed. You will find the yoke is easy and the burden is light. For he who breaks the crust of bread with his fellowman and lifts the cup to parched lips, does it as unto the Father . . . and this you have experienced.

Would you so desire to be one with us? We seek but those who have served. It is not man's physical position among his fellowman which interests us. It is what man is, in the Presence of God. What you are . . . not who you are. Again may I repeat, we open the gate along the path. The path leads to the conscious realization of the GREAT WHITE LIGHT OF THE FATHER. If you so desire to choose, we call you. You may so express yourself briefly and in so doing, you shall remember the words of Jesus the Christ, when he said, "Follow me and I shall make you fishers of men . . . Take up your cross and follow me."

And as He spake He called from all walks of life. And as He called they said unto him, "Ye EliBoni, I shall follow." Jesus the Christ lives . . . He beckons . . . He calls. He would make you a fisher of men.

And as they who answered His call in the fullness of heart, they answered, "Ye, Raboni Ye." Would you answer the call at this moment, dear heart? If so speak forth.

Student: "I choose, I choose the way. I am only the instrument."

You are a channel through which the fullness of God's Life flows. Remember my dear one, the bottle is not the wine. The cruet is not the oil. The chalice is not the wine. You are the chalice. You are the cruet in which the oil of Love rests. You are the candle stick which holds aloft the Lighted taper of Light. You are making no greater choice now than you have already made. It is but a desire of recognition and now harken you well.

You ascribe no vow to no man and your vow you make in the inner recesses of your own soul's consciousness with your God . . .

silently so. Let it now be done. Yes, dear heart. You shall have the strength, you shall have the courage. You shall not fail. You are one who bears the message of peace. One who shall not countenance strife among men of earth.

Here is another link in the golden chain of Love, another link which holds together the precious cargo of God. Remember, dear hearts, you have a precious cargo . . . peace to weary minds, comfort to throbbing breasts, oil to troubled hearts with the oil of Love. As you reckon time in days, weeks, months and years, you shall now know in greater measure than ever before, the true spiritual import of that prayer of Prayers . . . we shall create a good solid link.

You may repeat it silently as I audibly state it. . . . Meditating upon your Christship with the Father and your Brotherhood with your Elder Brother Jesus, the Christ . . . He who uttered that Prayer.

Bless each one of you, Bless you. You have wisely chosen to follow.

Goodnight, dear hearts, rejoice and be glad.

LOVE THY NEIGHBOR—OBEY THAT LAW AND LIVE

The humble Galilean Jesus, the Christ has said, "Come unto me all ye that are heavy laden and I shall give you rest . . . Come unto me ALL ye who are weary and heavy laden." Would you find rest, dear hearts?

Likewise has the Galilean said, "Take up thy cross and follow me, for he who loses his soul, shall find it." For man to lose himself in God is to find himself. Where does man live, but in the heart of God?

Where is God? Listen to the words of the lowly Nazarene, "Know ye not that the kingdom of God is within you?" How far can man stray from God? . . . BUT IN HIS THINKING . . . man is never lost. Though he would deny God, God does not forsake man.

Likewise the lovely Nazarene said, "Lo, I AM with you always." Faith, faith in God, is that by which man lives. Not a blind faith, a living faith. Let man of earth be ever mindful that he is the supremacy of God's creation. Let him in love, adore, revere, ever, the name and presence of the LIVING GOD. God is real, God is Life. All life is of God. Learn therefore, beloved of earth, all that which expresses life is of God.

Should there perchance be placed in your hand a cup which you would be asked to drink, and it be bitter, it is not of God. As you taste it, seek within the innermost depth of your heart's consciousness to find, *how you have filled the cup,* then remember the words of the Galilean, "Come unto me all ye who are weary and heavy laden, for 'I' shall give you rest." For it was He who said to the Father, "And if it be thy will, O Father, may this cup pass from me? But not my will be done Father, Thy will be done, for it is in this cause I have come; it is in this cause you have sent me."

There is no bitterness in life, but what man of earth, HAS BROUGHT UPON HIMSELF. Let us listen to the reasoning of Job, when he said, "The thing I have feared, has come upon me." Fear is direct contradiction to God. God is not fear. God is not unjust. God knows no enmity.

Here on your physical plane of life, dawns the hour when man

153

shall be friendly with his neighbor, when he shall hold against his neighbor no ill will. Let man of earth ever extend his hand in graciousness. Strife shall only come to an end, dear hearts, when man has learned to say and truthfully so, "You are my brother, you are my sister."

Jesus the Christ said this and he so continues to speak FOR HE LIVES. Said the Christ, "If you come to the altar with thy gift and remember in thy heart, that thou holdest ought against thy brother, leave thy gift at the altar and make thy peace with thy brother. Then come to the altar and offer thy gift, with all thy might, with all thy soul, love thy God and love thy neighbor as thyself." . . . THIS IS THE IMMUTABLE LAW OF GOD. This is the path of Peace, dear hearts . . . no other path to be trod.

Likewise hath the Nazarene said, "Hath not God caused the sun to shine upon, and the rain to fall upon, the just and the unjust alike." When shall the man who calls himself the Advocate of God, speak in Truth? When shall creed and dogmas be set aside and the story of God's Love told to man of earth? He who stands in the temple before God and advocate for man, shall proclaim the Love of God, shall proclaim the Truth of the Resurrected Christ.

We hear man of earth say that the earth is sick with sin and strife, chaos and woe and the antagonist to Truth says in his heart, "Why shall this be? Your religion is false. There is no God." We say to you, *there is a God . . . God is a living reality . . . Jesus, the Christ lives . . . a living reality.* It is but the fool in his heart who sayeth, "There is no God."

God expresses through man as God expresses through every manifest beauty in life . . . "Behold the lily of the field, it spins not, neither does it reap. Yet Solomon in all his glory was not so beautifully arrayed." Behold the tiny wild flower, blooming along the side of life's highway, covered with dust, grime of the road, yet it expresses the beauty of God. It smiles into the tired weary countenance of the wayfarer. Would that man lived as the tiny wild flower, ever obedient to God's Law. Expressing the Love of the Creator.

As true as the words are spoken, as true as they are written, harken ye well now. God is no respecter of man. God's eye is on the man and woman, who lives in the brothels of society, as is his eyes upon the man or woman who lives in high places. Though man may deny God and blaspheme God, God continues to speak and say, "No, my child, No, be still and know that . . . 'I AM' . . . God." Set aside the bitter cup you have created for yourself my child. Here I give to you the chalice of love, it has been standing on the altar in your heart ever since the beginning but you have beheld it not, for you would not see."

There is no mystery in God, dear hearts. Do you doubt that you have hands and feet? Do you doubt that you breathe? God is a greater reality than hands and feet. The very breath you breathe, is the reality of the living God. For the breath you breathe IS the breath of God. Live, dear hearts, live, live in the love of God. Love your neighbor as your self . . . live. Learn to live with God. Seek within the inner recesses of your heart's consciousness, God is there . . . LISTEN IN THE SILENCE . . . LISTEN AND YOU SHALL HEAR GOD SPEAK.

Behold beauty all about you and you shall see God in manifestation. God is not afar off, within your hearts consciousness. Man of earth has coined these words and very true they are, "God is closer than hands and feet, closer than the hair in your head." How beautifully spoken. Believe dear hearts, BELIEVE . . . ONLY BELIEVE. And you shall live in the freedom of God's Love. Learn to bless your every possession with the realization, that it is of God. As you go to your couch of rest at night, the couch upon which you lay your physical temple, in your last waking hours learn to say, *"Father I thank Thee for Life."* As you arise your body in the morning, learn to say, *"Father I thank Thee for Light."*

Life is abundant, it is everlasting unto everlasting; more precious is life; more precious is the soul; than the physical temple in which life manifests. With that Truth your physical temple shall respond to the life of God . . . God first, last and always.

Listen to the words of the Nazarene, "Lo, I AM with you always." I AM . . . God in manifestation. We are happy for this opportunity to visit with you and we have so spoken dear hearts, that when the hour is at hand, that your fellowman asks the question of you, "What makes you so happy, what makes your countenance radiate in the manner which it does?" You may answer truthfully, "I have found the LIVING God."

Bless each one of you a thousand times ten thousand, Faith, dear hearts. All things are possible with God. Faith . . . faith in God. Faith in God is faith in yourself . . . faith in God . . . Faith in your self is faith in your fellowman. Go forth and live, no fear . . . no fear . . . no fear. Dear hearts, no fear, no fear.

Good night.

LORD'S PRAYER

We are happy, we rejoice with you, we give thanks. You, dear ones, now understand the word's of the Galilean when he said, "Lo I am with you always." There is but one presence, as you know it. It ever abounds in Power and in Truth. And it becomes that part of man as man so accepts it to be. It is for that reason we continue to reason with you, dear ones, to be ever positive. As you already know one does not speak until they have so formulated their words in thinking.

When man learns THE Power, he expresses in saying, "I AM" he shall *never speak in negation* of the Creative Principle in Life. For you will remember the Galilean said to the Pharisees, "Before Abraham was . . . I AM." I AM and "Our Father" . . . Power . . . Peace . . . Plenty.

The physical body is to receive every worthy consideration, for it is the temple of the living God. It shall never meet with disregard in man's thinking, for likewise the Galilean said, "Keep ye therefore clean and undefiled the temple of the loving God." It is well for external cleanliness and we are agreed with it, it is well that man takes what he calls pride, the manner in which he clothes the physical temple. But the GREAT CLEANLINESS IS IN MAN'S THINKING. Desire, dear hearts . . . desire. When he desires to live and sincerely desires to live, the physical body shall respond to that desire.

Among the many Beatitudes, you will find this one, "Blessed are the pure in heart, for they shall see God." How does man see God? Where is the heart of man? How is man pure in his heart? . . . In his thinking, and with the purity of desire to live and to express God, the physical temple radiates health. The very countenance radiates with the Life of God. It is in that manner that man catches a Glimpse of God.

"I am God's child. I am ONE with God." What shall man disregard, in the creation of the physical temple? Not one consideration. Who created the physical temple? . . . God, therefore the physical temple is not just gross matter, as man has so recognized it to be.

157

You, dear ones, who are working with the elements of nature, you are familiar with radio activity are you not? Why do you find it? From whence does it come? Is it not POWER? Since God has created the physical temple, *God has left a part of God's self in every cell and atom of that temple.* It needs must be for it, if it were not so, Man's prayer for the restoring of health to the physical temple could not be. Each cell of the physical body is alive, it responds to both negative thinking and to constructive thinking.

"I am life, I am health, I am the perfection of the Living God . . . I love life, I love God . . . my breath is the breath of God." What is man doing when he so speaks? He is but declaring his oneness with the Father.

"OUR Father, who art in Heaven." What is man saying? Man is not pleading, man is not begging, it is not a vain supplication. It is a dynamic degree of recognition with God.

"Our Father." The Father of what? The Father of whom? The *Father of all that which expresses LIFE.* It is man's recognition of not only his oneness with the Father . . . Co-heir ON the throne of Life . . . *ruler with the Father* in the Father's Kingdom, but it is likewise recognition, of his oneness with all mankind.

"Hallowed be thy name," An expression of Love, adoration, but above all a declaration of acceptance.

"Thy Kingdom come, not ON earth . . . IN earth, as it is IN Heaven." There is no separation in God. *God knows nothing about segregation, no limitation.* For man to say "ON earth" that power could be isolated to some small remote corner of the Universe. "In earth" dear hearts, "As it is in Heaven." And the physical body is of the earth earthy, but it is alive with the power of God. Remember God created it, it is part of the great atom of the Universe. It Lives, it needs must be, for it is the dwelling place of God.

Therefore when man makes the statement, "I am life, I am health, I am power." He is speaking to the minute cells of the physical body, which are waiting to hear the voice of the Creator. Man is God's child. Man is perfect spiritual being. Man has never changed, he may lose his way, but listen, dear hearts, *as a tiny spark of the eternal flame, the spark left its seat of perfection, in perfection . . . and it returns in the same perfection, for perfection is never destroyed.*

You, dear ones, are working with the elements of nature, the elements of God are proving that to be Truth. It is in that manner, you shall prove to the rejector of Truth, that God is.

To a dear one present . . . you prayed a prayer as you walked through the valley and your prayer was a prayer of Thanksgiving. You thanked God for Life. You remember do you not? And as you did, Life became manifest. Listen with us, dear heart, there is no past to behold, all things become new and we rejoice with you. You are God's child and as you continue to declare your oneness with God . . . IN God, the physical temple shall again express the radiant life it did when you first claimed it. And in speaking to this dear one we are speaking to each one of you. Man cannot live the life of his fellowman and we are agreed with that.

But the Sage of ancient age said this, "Thou art thy brother's keeper." What is the meaning of the words, "thy brother's keeper"? Love expresses perfect order in God . . . *love is the Christ principle of life.* Therefore the Nazarene said, "Love ye one another."

Yes, it is true. Man of earth cannot live the life of his brother, but he who possesses Light, can illumine the dark road of his brother. Therefore he becomes his brother's keeper, "Cast thy bread upon the waters and after many days it shall return unto you and you shall find it." Man finds the bread he cast upon the waters.

In the pattern of prayer which the Nazarene gave unto man to use, man has learned to say this, "Give us this day our daily bread." Bread . . . symbolizing the Spiritual sustenance of Life. Let us examine the statement. There is but ONE day in the realm of God. Likewise has the Nazarene said, "Man lives not by bread alone, but by every word which proceedeth forth from the mouth of God." May we try and weave the statements together.

"Give us THIS DAY" . . . not tomorrow, not days, weeks, months, in that which man has learned to call the future . . . *"This day" God's eternal day, "Give us this day our daily bread." That is not a plea, it is not a lame petition, it is a statement of confidence. To whom?*

"Our Father who art in Heaven." It is denying the limitation of mortal mind and it is pointing the blade of the plow of life into fertile soil of understanding and turning over new soil, as it were.

And the statement is good, fertile, healthy seed dropped in the new soil.

Bread . . . the Spiritual sustenance of Life, provides the needs at hand and the need at hand grows and as it does, man knows no want. For the Nazarene has said, "That which you have need of, the Father knoweth before you ask and as ye ask in secret . . . which is in silence . . . the Father rewardeth thee openly."

Listen, dear hearts, I AM power . . . I AM health, I am the Glory of God in manifestation . . . I am the resurrection and the Life . . . I am the perfect likeness of God . . . *That is the Bread of Life, dear hearts. That is spiritual sustenance.*

Likewise the Nazarene has said, "If the son ask the Father for bread, shall the Father give him a stone? And if the son ask the Father for a fish shall He give him a serpent?" Ask the Father, dear hearts, there are no stones, no serpents, in the Father's storehouse of Infinite supply.

Let us go one step further with the prayer, "Give us this day our daily bread" and said the Nazarene "forgive us our debtors as we forgive our debtors." The paying of the claim, dear hearts. Forgiveness is expressing Love and Love meets every need.

For the Galilean has said, "Love ye one another . . . Love even those who despitefully use you." For we have heard one of you say, "I forgive you, I forgive you, I forgive you." Well spoken, the Blessing of God is with you, What is man saying when he says, "I forgive you."

Let us go back to man's recognition of God in the prayer, "Our Father." Man's recognition of his sonship with the God and the Brotherhood of man. God is All Forgiving and when man says, "I forgive you." He is saying this, "I am giving God's Love to you; for the error you committed in blindness I forgive." I, the oneness of Life. Every kindly word, every kindly act, every kindly deed says, "I forgive you." Every smile of Love says, "I forgive you, I forgive you." It is then that man's inner chamber becomes deplete of all malice, all desire to rule physically so. It is then that the Father expresses in wholeness, the giving of the Old for the New. "For behold ALL things have become new."

We love you, we love you, we love you dear hearts and though it may be physically, as you would say, impossible to place your hand in the hand of your fellowman, when you so desire to do, you have a spiritual hand, it is the Hand of God. Reach it forth with your benediction of Love. You shall find that you have been your brothers keeper. Love is the keeper . . . Love . . . Love . . . Love. It is not the age of the body, it is the BEAUTY OF THE SOUL.

Dear ones, be as links in a chain of Love. You shall know the meaning of the words, "I desireth not sacrifice, moreover mercy," said Jehovah. Love is mercy, mercy is Love, Love and mercy knows no sacrifice. Now is the hour of the rapture, not in that which man sings of, as the "Sweet bye and bye." Now, is man caught up in the rapture of rejoicing . . . now, he knows of the true meaning of the closing words of the Prayer, "For thine is the Kingdom and the Power and the Glory for ever, world without end."

Bless each one of you.

KEEP YOUR EYE SINGLE UNTO THE LIGHT

O Lord of Hosts
May my eyes wide open be
To see the Christ in every man of earth I meet.
O Lord of Hosts
May I rise from the small confines of self
To the selfless life in Thee.
O Lord of Hosts
May I resign-ed be
To speak in Love . . . the Love
Which Thou dost behold in me.
O Lord of Hosts
May I grasp the hand of my fellowman
In all sincerity
And seek no claim of reward
But that of Love from Thee.
And with the Christ, who in Jesus dwelt,
May I too learn to say,
"And I, if I be lifted up
Shall draw all mankind to me."
In selflessness,
O Lord of Hosts,
This prayer I pray;
A Christlike Christian
to ever be.
     Amen—Amen—Amen

Greetings:

As so often we have endeavored to discuss with you, dear ones, we make reference this evening. There is no time. There is but one day and that day is to be lived wholly DEDICATED TO GOD, whose day it is. How often we hear man of earth say, "I would be Christ-like." And it is well for man to desire to be Christ-like. For there is but one day and that is known to man of earth as today.

For man of earth to be a blessing to his fellowman is the first requisite of the Christ life. And when man's desire in selflessness is so dedicated, his pattern of living shall become humbly selfless. We have likewise reasoned in this manner; Life is beautiful, Life is sweet, Life is complete. Unto each man of earth is allotted a certain portion of Life's great pattern. He but lives his own portion of Life's pattern and is not accountable to himself or to God for the manner in which his fellowman lives his portion of life's pattern. That too is Christ-like.

Each teacher in their time, unto their own people, exemplified to a degree the Christ of God. Man of today is no different than any other teacher. *He of today who has forsaken the carnal path of life and has espoused that which he calls the Christian path of Life, has so made the choice because of experiences encountered in previous Life experiences.*

MAN MUST GROW. A choice made today shall be kept as inviolate, when tomorrow becomes today, as it was in the hour the choice was made. We have repeatedly mentioned that we make no distinction between one from the other of man of earth. If it were so, in your vernacular of speech, it would become difficult for us to call, that man might choose to follow. The Nazarene said and continues to say now, in the fullness of spirit, "Seek ye first, the Kingdom of God." *It was the Christ Spirit of God which uttered that statement through Jesus of Nazareth. And that self same Christ Spirit lives, as you shall continue to live, after your mortal coil has released you into the vastness from which you came.*

"Seek ye first the Kingdom of God and all these things shall be added unto you." Humility of purpose is the golden link in the golden chain of life. Man receives no other reward in living Life's Pattern than that which HE SEEKS. There are many men of notable mention whose likenesses hang in museums known as Halls of Fame. And they so sought to have their likenesses therein placed. All that which they sought to do was for self, vain glory. They had forgotten to seek the kingdom of God. And all who pass as spectators through the hall of fame, behold but a likeness, emblazened upon a canvas in a Gilded Frame.

And well could we of the Council have had our likenesses hanging in Hall's of Fame, here on this mundane sphere of life, and accepted that reward. There is a greater reward than to be eulogized by man of earth. He who seeks to be eulogized is neglecting the priceless gift, the priceless attainment in life . . . The Kingdom of God.

How often have we repeated, let there be peace. *God is not the author of confusion. God is the author of Peace.* Man shall never know peace, individually at least, until he has found the Kingdom of God. And the Kingdom of God is within. It is the highest possible state in consciousness; clean, wholesome, genuine kindness is a Christ-like quality . . . humble, not expressed with the expectation of vain glory. For the Galilean said, "Be ye not like they who stand upon the street corners to be heard of men, for they have their reward." He knew in the everyday life, in the everyday life of man of earth, in that which is referred to as business, TRUE SUCCESS IS ACHIEVED BY HUMILITY. And the more humble one pursues the path of success, the greater and the more genuine is that success.

That, the Apostle Paul understood when he wrote the words, "Be ye therefore not given over unto outward appearances, for hath not God written his law in their hearts?" Woe betide unto the man of earth who would dare to question the sincerity or pronounce that of insincerity upon his fellowman. Who in the mortal coil is of that authority? It is not the outward appearance which reveals the true worth and value of that which is secretly emblazened upon life's scroll, in the heart's consciousness of man.

The Galilean likewise said, "Therefore let not the right hand know what the left hand doeth." Woe betide unto the individual who would, as sowing seed, broadcast their virtue and their deeds as dealt to their fellowman. For as the canvas in the Gilded Frame in the Hall of Fame, they have their reward.

HUMILITY IS POWER. Within your keeping you have a lesson wherein we discussed with you that it was unfair to exercise the rule of tyranny. In your public or daily papers it has become known to you the results of tyrannical power, not only in the country in which you live, but in other countries, Religiously so, as well as political, it has brought forth what? Confusion!

It shall be a lesson unto man in living that portion of Life's Pattern allotted to him. For the confusion was born in the womb of men seeking religious and political acclaim . . . power. And it is needless for we of the Council to mention the destructiveness which follows in the wake of such desired power. Man is free. We of the Council have never demanded, neither have we ever sent forth a command, and neither do we reject one whom we have called, and through that calling, who has chosen to follow and perchance has stopped to loiter along the path.

As we have mentioned previously, we repeat. To we of the Council it is not who a man is . . . it is what a man is. And it is ever our endeavor and shall ever be, to aid and assist man of earth to overcome the mistakes of that known as the past. That the gray, drab, carnal threads of his portion of life's pattern may become glistening, golden threads.

We have asked you, dear ones, may we ask again, apply yourselves, dear hearts, to the receptiveness of the Illumined Christ-Power of which you are, that you may be able to receive and to know, independent and irrespective of any other channel. Know the truth and the truth shall set you free.

Remember well the story as narrated in your Holy Writ of Jesus the Christ and His disciples, when He said, "I must needs depart for a season that ye may increase." Seasons are but the lengthening of the day in which man lives. It is but one day. "Prepare ye the way while ye are yet in it," said the Galilean. "Agree with thy adversary quickly while thou are yet in the way with him." Agree? . . . Yes.

Recognition of the Christ Power which always rises above adversity. Behold the Light while the Light shineth. Walk not in its shadow, moreover in the brightness of the Light.

Man casteth his own shadow. "If thine eye be single unto the Light," said the Nazarene, "how great shall thy light be, but if thine eye be single unto the darkness, how great shall the darkness be." Walk in the brightness of the Light and as you walk Life's Path be not afraid. For where there is Light there can be no darkness. Speak not one word of which regret shall become its child. Speak lovingly . . . kindly. The truth of God imparted through the Christ consciousness is a priceless gift to be treasured and cannot be weighed with gold of the mundane sphere.

If that which we have spoken of in the past be forgotten, do not forget that statement. God's alabaster box of ointment cannot be bought with earthly gold. The Nazarene understood this when Judas said, "This woman wasteth the ointment upon thy feet." God's word is priceless. God's word is the FLAWLESS DIAMOND.

And as we have previously mentioned, may we repeat, in whatever manner you raise your hand in consciousness say, "This I do unto God." For mind you well, there is a God and the very breath you breathe is proof sufficient that GOD IS.

Let your prayer ever be, "From the unreal to the real . . . from darkness unto light . . . from the unreality of death to the reality of life." "Prepare thy self while thou art in the way." You will then understand the blessedness of true service to your God . . . Yes.

The parched dry grass which burns beneath the heat of the sun's rays, knows the absence of the rain and he who enjoys the beauty of the sun, understands its beneficence, when it is hidden from him by the denseness of the overshadowing clouds. And he who enjoys the warmth of the sun's rays, understands the beneficence of the sun's warmth, only when the cold chilling blast of the frigid wind strikes his cheeks.

Walk in the light, a dedicated life, not only to your God but with your God. So live today that when today becomes tomorrow, it shall reflect the beauty of today as you have so lived it. Speak that when the echo of your voice returns, it shall be sweet music unto your ears and not cause tears of regret to fall from your eyes upon parched cheeks.

Good night, dear hearts. Walk in the light and you will live in the light.

We love you, we love you. Bless your every endeavor. "Though I speak with the tongues of angels and have not love, it profiteth me nothing," said the Apostle Paul and he added, "And now abideth Faith, Hope and Love, these three, but the greatest of these is Love."

That is the Christian way of living life's pattern . . . that is the true hall of true undeniable fame.

Good night, Good night.

REBIRTH IS MAN'S DESIRE

Thoughts of Love are lighted tapers upon man's altar;
Thoughts of Love are angels, Heaven born and Heaven sent
From within the realm of man's thinking, in his devotion with his
    God.
Love sends the angels on their way
Love wings which carry the angels to man . . . man's fellowman;
Love, Love are angels sent from the Heaven within.
Let there be peace, let there be peace, and man with angels
Shall in Heaven dwell. Amen.

As always, each opportunity to visit with you, dear ones, is indeed
a very happy experience by we of the Council. There is peace and let
no man of earth, in his mortal confusion inform you to the contrary.
There is peace and the sooner man desires peace, covets peace, with
all his might and all his Love and pays no heed to that which he hears
to the contrary, the sooner confusion shall be swirled up in its native
nothingness.

We have frequently stated that God is birthless, ageless, deathless.
Man, the image of God, is birthless, ageless and deathless. Rebirth *is
not mandatory by any established law of God* . . . Rebirth is man's
choice. Since God is birthless, man his image, is likewise birthless.
How then rebirth? Does it appear to be a mystery to you?

It is the flesh that is born it is BORN because it is B-O-R-N-E
by the Power of Spirit. You will remember we of the Council saying,
"What is the sum aggregate, total of that which God created, of
that which God made?

You will likewise remember we reasoned, that *the image* of *God is
spirit . . . not a spirit.* And that which God made out of that which
God created was but the physical habiliment or the dwelling place,
the conveyance on the mundane sphere of life, for the created likeness of God. Therefore, it is reasonable to know that all that which
expresses life bears the image of God. Be it animal, vegetable or
mineral, it bears the image of God.

Why is man here in this present incarnation? The path of life becomes, in your vernacular of speech, UNFINISHED BUSINESS. *Never become deceived that the law of reincarnation or rebirth, is a manifestation of retrogression.* Man moves on. May we repeat . . . each experience is a lesson and each lesson well learned, is an experience *well earned.*

We hear man of earth say, "I have had nothing but difficulty, ever since I can remember." Of course he is speaking about his memory in the present incarnation, for if he were to remember each incarnation through which he passed, he would not wonder why he is having all the trouble he thinks he has, and *that is progression,* please, not retrogression.

Experience . . . lesson . . . experience well earned. It therefore behooves man to express as much love and kindness as his understanding of Life's pattern permits him so to do. You shall never be called upon to share a kindness, only because of the fact that it is enabling you, as it were, to untie knots of the past. If it is but in silence say, "God Bless you my friend, you are my brother; God bless you."

If you are unable to share your worldly goods, a blessing you can give. You can find many angels in your Heaven, for the angelic hosts of Heaven are sweet, kind, loving, precious thoughts. God Bless you, my friend. A sweet smile expresses an angel. Would you live in Heaven with your God? Remember, it was you and only you who in the hour of sex congress who said, "There is a body coming forth out of that act, I shall claim it. For the man and woman in the act attract me with the weight of desire which is necessary for me to claim a body necessary to experience the lessons, necessary to release me from the bondage of Unfinished Business." Birth, Birth, it is man's will, man's desire to choose a body and he bears it forth.

B-O-R-N-E . . . borne on the pinions of desire. Should your sojourn in your present physical body be such that the record is not clear, what shall be the impelling desire for another physical temple and where shall be the man and woman you shall seek, whereby you shall claim that body?

The very manner in which you are living life's pattern as it is allotted to you, your portion of life's pattern . . . the very manner in which you are living it is Now creating that desire which shall bring you to the man and woman, where you shall make your choice, because of the attraction in their mental structure to continue to work out unfinished business.

We hear man of earth say, "Poor child, they have come here against their will." If that statement alone were pondered upon, it would be sufficient to promote, what man of earth calls Good Will and kindness. But no child as children are called . . . comes against their will. Their will brings them, if you please, therefore, the bargain is equal between parent and child, using your vernacular of earth.

Angels of kindness, thoughts of Love, when you experience a difficulty as you understand a difficulty, with some relative, as you understand relationship, or friend as you understand friendship. Or wherever you encounter that which you call difficulty . . . stop and ask yourself this question, "Where did I start this ball rolling, that it is now making itself evident in my path?"

You will say to me and you will be justified in so stating, "I have been good to people, I have been kind and what have I received in return for it." With what are you going to become concerned? You are not going to be selfish in the manner in which you complete your UNFINISHED BUSINESS, are you? Lest through selfishness you create more unfinished business. What shall you do with the one who has returned unkindness for your kindness? Each experience is a lesson well learned and each lesson well learned is an experience *well earned.*

You will bless the one, who has returned unkindness for kindness, for in so doing, you are bringing into manifestation the Truth of the statement of the Master Nazarene, when he said, "Agree with thine adversary, while thou art yet in the way with him, lest he deliver thee unto the officer and the officer unto the judge, and the judge will cast ye into prison, and ye shall not come forth therefrom till thou has paid the last farthing."

The officer . . . possessiveness; the judge . . . the judgment of the very act in consciousness; the prison house . . . the confinement in consciousness to the acts committed; and the payment of the debts . . . REBIRTH AFTER REBIRTH, UNTIL THE UNFINISHED IS FINISHED.

Rejoice and be happy that you are here in the physical temple and be mindful of this, that the physical temple is made of all that which God created, and that which God created was good. Do you have to experience rebirth? That is your choice. What will you do about it? Why are you interested in seeking the Christ Light of God? Why are you not spending the hour of this your evening, seeking some physical mundane pleasure, idling away your precious time. Why are you here? Why are you here?

You . . . You the Spirit, seeking liberation from the prison house, you have the farthing and you are willing to pay for it. A spiritual farthing, you are crying, "ABA Father, ABA Father." And the Father says, *"Be still my child, and Know that I AM God . . . I AM God." Are you going to continue to say, "I am worthless, I cannot do it, I can never hope to do that." I AM is God, you are going to say, "all Power is given unto me . . . in Heaven and in earth . . . I AM has sent me . . . I am God's image . . . I am now free."*

FORSAKING THE OLD FOR THE NEW

The heat of the day has passed,
The chill of the night kisses the warm earth.
The dew arises but to fall
Upon the petal of the rose and the leaf as well.
Hush are the busy marts of life,
Stars in the sky do twinkle and shine
And the moon its silvery light does cast.
And the dewdrops; as the stars they sparkle,
Mingled with the light of the sun and the silvery moon.
Still is the night and rests; still is the night and rests.
Peace comes to the troubled breasts,
The weary heart rests. Peace and all is well
Hush is the night and all is well.
All is well. So mote it be.

Greetings dear hearts, let there be peace, peace. Let there be peace.
When hands are joined in love, so likewise are hearts love entwined
. . . love entwined. There are no years, it is but a day. And the day in
which hands are clasped and hearts entwined in love, that day holds
no regret. There is peace where there is love. Love knows no sorrow
and never causes that to happen which brings regrets.

The rose blooms forth in beauty and it has no regrets when its
petals fall. For it has expressed the undeniable Presence of God. The
tiny flower, as it grows along the highway of life knows no lonesome-
ness, for it is not alone, it is all one with God. As the wafts of air
touch the tiny bloom it nods its head to the weary footsore wayfarer
and says, "You are not alone, you are all one with God . . . all one
. . . not alone."

The rain descends upon the babbling brook and each drop falls
and as it does it says, "We are all one, we left you but a season ago,
yet are not separated, for as we left you, we knew we would return.
We are back again, but to return from that source of life which we
have just left."

The rays of the sun leaves the great oneness of the great sun, but

171

they are not lost, they return but to reach man of earth in that time which man of earth calls his tomorrow. The moonbeams dance upon the oceans deep upon the seas, lakes and brooks, but they are not lost. For when night falls on man's tomorrow, they shall again dance upon the seas, oceans and lakes and brooks.

Alone? No, dear hearts, ALL ONE, never alone. That which man accepts in love, at the moment he accepts in love, he shall prepare to release in love. There is no possession in love. Nature is not possessive. If nature were possessive, what would man do for that which he calls seasons of his year? Nature rejoices and as it rejoices, it yields to man that which God has created.

Man, O man of earth, learn natures scroll of love. It is written in the language of action, not in words to be misinterpreted; written upon an eternal everlasting scroll. Spring comes and summer follows. Autumn comes and winter follows, but to be swallowed up again when Spring returns, it is the language in action.

Live, O man of earth by the scroll which nature has emblazened before thee. O man of earth, you are of nature as the flower along life's highway, as the rose in the well-tended garden . . . as the sparkling dewdrop . . . as the rays of the sun . . . as the moonbeams O man of earth, you are a part of nature. Rejoice and be exceeding glad, rejoice. Yes there is a wedded life, wedded in the Holy Sacred bonds of nature. A most intricate part of *All there is,* in that which man had learned to call life. *Love is sacred and it seeks not for deception. It knows nought of suspicion and therefore weeps not when night falls and rest comes.*

The last enemy to be overcome is death. Death, there is no death. Life is everlasting unto everlasting. What is the meaning of this statement, "The last enemy to be overcome is death." What man or woman of earth is happy when they have not peace of mind? *Overcoming that which causes mental distress is overcoming a death.*

Unpleasantnesses, as man of earth experiences them, are enemies to happiness. Happiness is found on the heavenly laden table, which the Psalmist spoke of when he said, "Thou preparest a table before me in the presence of mine enemies." How is that table spread and with what? Each man and woman of earth prepares that table in consciousness. It is laden with all that which love expresses.

There are many losses, so to speak, far greater than the loss of a physical companionship, for life is everlasting. And as we have so often times said, "There is no separation." Friendship bathed in the Power of Love cannot be lost. Often man of earth disregards a friendship, but when he or she who would be friends, is moved by the power of love, that friendship of love never dies and so along life's highway becomes recognized. It has always expressed itself. It has not been beheld by the one who rejected it.

Will you remember the story of two men as narrated in your Holy Writ. One was referred to a rich man, but he was not rich for the reason he did not recognize his spiritual riches, yet it rested buried in his consciousness. But he was numbered among the wealthy people of his country and because of his wealth, he had power and authority, physically so. The other man was a certain Lazarus at the gate to the city. His body was covered with sores and the dogs licked his sores in kindness. And the wealthy man passed, and the certain Lazarus was asking alms and he asked of the wealthy man and the wealthy man refused him and spat upon him. And as the story continues, the certain Lazarus continued to beg at the city gates and the wealthy man died.

And you will remember the wealthy man cried from the depths of Hell and said, "Cannot Lazarus wet my lips?" He calls for the one he rejected and spat upon. Hell . . . where is it? It is but a condition of man's thinking. But the wealthy man discovered compassion in Lazarus. For Lazarus did not rebuke him, when the wealthy man refused him and spat upon him. Therefore the wealthy man in his anguish asked, "Cannot Lazarus wet my parched lips?" What is the meaning of the story?

Spiritual Love is never lost, but it can be overlooked when mortal or mundane power becomes the underlying quest of man. But love does not die, it cannot. It is upon the table spread before man, in the presence of his enemies in the quest for power. Might is an enemy which does not recognize the bounty and abundance upon the table. Lazarus was rich for he possessed spiritual love.

What was the lot of Lazarus in the previous incarnation? Just that of the wealthy man whom he met at the gate of the city and for that reason, the incarnation in which Lazarus lived, did not bestow upon him earthly or physical wealth but he found spiritual riches, as even the one, who spat upon him, found it.

We hear man of earth make this statement quite frequently, "I know I have committed error. I know I have not been just as kindly as I should have been, but I cannot reach for the hand of the one whom I have rejected. I do not feel spiritually strong enough to ask forgiveness." And that, dear hearts, is not necessary. Love never demands forgiveness. How then shall man of earth overcome in his thinking, the LAW OF FORGIVENESS which he has become conscious of? *Well, he shall forgive himself. How? He shall give up the old for the new . . . give for . . . forgive.*

When the Light, regardless of how faintly it flickers, when the Light brings the illumination and man of earth would cry, "Cannot Lazarus wet my parched lips?" It is then he or she who will, beholding the Light, realizing all the mistakes of the past, say "I give the old for the new . . . I FORGIVE." And when in consciousness that has been accomplished, the one who has silently loved and has silently prayed, is moved to answer the summons. Why? There is no separation in God. Spiritually man is one and love is power. Forgive . . . give up the old for the new. And the last enemy shall be overcome. Death to man's ideas, inspiration, aspiration, hopes . . . that enemy shall be overcome. Again man shall come into the conscious realization, the fulfillment of his ideas, his inspiration, his aspiration and his hopes. *Love is the undeniable error impelling power of the universe in which man lives.*

There is no parting, it cannot be. Time is not. Distance cannot be. Memory, O memory holds its cherished reflections. Love is eternal destiny.

Bless each one of you, a thousand times ten thousand. The last enemy SHALL BE OVERCOME. Bye the Bye.

READING LIFE'S SCROLLS

Forever rise with silvery fleece the sun.
It shines, though man does not see
And so the stars when the sky o'ercasts, they twinkle in the sky.
Man of earth, look thou within, there light is, no turbulent sea
No storm clouds on that horizon rolls,
Look thou within, and see.
Why seekest thou, around about, on that which thou call "without?"
When all that is, lies within the chamber of thy soul, devout.
That which man creates with hands shall vanish
It is but transient in its flight.
But within thy soul there thou shall find that which God has given
    thee for life.
There is no death, as you well know, for ofttimes have you heard that
    life moves on as an endless sea.
There is no death, it cannot be.
What woe of earth possesses man? Why struggles he with fear and
    doubt?
For all that which he struggles with, he finds without, and not
    within.
Within, there is no din. Peace and harmony reigns within.
The printed page cannot reveal the vast expanse of life's great scroll.
For on the printed page man finds but half life's story told.
There is a book that man shall read, 'tis written in his soul.
Who is the author of that book? None but man who writes the scroll.
What fault shall man of earth then find with those whom he calls
    his fellowman?
Why shall man of earth demand when he himself cannot command
    his own life soul to plan.
There is no bondage but what man creates. Let man of earth then so
    accept that which becomes his just desert. By every act of his
    own will . . . unregenerate will.
When in love man does arise unto the supernal heights of God.
He then shall know the text contained upon the page unwritten by
    hand.

Thought, words, acts, and deeds. The pen, the ink, is it that ascribes the lesson man shall learn?

He, the author, soon forgets. Let not his memory be short lived,

For memory never dies but gives back to its author all there inscribed.

Pluck not the beam from thy brother's eye, and behold not the mote within thine own.

Wherein does all perfection lie? Within the heart of gold, the heart of God within man's soul.

Struggle not with adversity, moreover say, "What hast thou with me?"

"Art thou my child? Did I thee bear?" It surely is

For those wouldst not come to me to share lest in my womb of thinking I did thee conceive.

I shall bear, as I bear along life's path and cease no more to struggle;

I shall erase until at last life's lesson I shall have learned.

Behold the lily of the fields. Its whiteness the purity of God reveals,

And from its very inner part, pastel yellow, or thereabouts, the symbols of God's gold.

Where are the roots, the lily thereof, but in the sod, as black and drab?

Yet from its blackness comes the white arising above that which man likens unto night.

Black soil of the mundane sphere, yet from its depths God's beauty comes.

Fret not your hearts over the earth; trod well your path

You, as the lily, can express the whiteness of your soul,

And then your brother, whom you have blessed, can say; when you the mundane sphere have left,

"He kept the whiteness of his soul and o'er him man of earth wept."

God is Love. One God, One Universe, one soul ruler of the universe . . . God,

One law, the law of God. One sole interpreter of the law . . . man. Look well within thy soul;

There revealed you shall find the law of life, not on the printed page. Which perchance has come because of strife.

Harken within thine inner self. *Thou art thine own teacher!*

Dear hearts, you are joined together in a blessed endeavor. It has never been, it is not now, and never shall be, our aim or purpose to leave one word which shall cause you, dear ones, or anyone with whom we speak, to conceive the idea of deception. In God there is no secrecy, and with man of earth who accepts God, he shall not deceive himself. And to those here on your mundane sphere of life, who either through ignorance of the fact, or through deliberate denial, do not behold their identity with God. Therefore, we say, put not upon the lips of he or she who knoweth not how to speak the Truth of God, that which, in their ignorance, willfully or otherwise, may desecrate.

Unto each one of you now the hour comes, when you shall become, as you of earth understand the word, active. Therefore, that which nature reveals nestle within your heart's consciousness, lest it be misunderstood by they who know not the living God.

Therefore may we repeat, within the sacred confines of your heart's consciousness hold fast the revealings which are now to come to pass, to come into being. For, the hour is at hand, and we are desirous that each of you become acquainted with that which man of earth has learned to call the wonders of nature. Keep it nestled within your bosom, as it were. There let it grow. Let it grow there and come forth with the radiance, beauty, purity, of the lily of the field.

It now becomes necessary for we of the Council, unseen by physical eyes, to reach forth for collaborators, for remember, the oak has no firmness in the soil with but one root. It has many roots. Therefore, as it becomes tall, stalwart, sturdy, that its branches reach out as far and further than its roots, each one of you shall have a duty to perform. We are well aware that each one of you has daily duties to perform. And we would not demand that of your time, as you understand time, unduly so, in the service of we of the Council. We endeavor to be consistent, please. Let man of earth, therefore, be consistent with his fellowman. Consistency, one with another, is the foundation stone of that which man has learned to call harmony. And where there is harmony love is expressed.

Below the surface of the earth nature lives in harmony. Above the surface of the earth nature lives in harmony, for the reason that that which is below the surface of the earth, and that which is above the surface of the earth has learned to read the unprinted page. Man has yet to learn to read the unprinted page. "Would you know life abundant, love doubled for all you give? There is a means no surer than helping someone to live." And how can man of earth help another to live unless he himself his first learned the lesson of life and how to live? *Look within.* There you will find inscribed the eternal scroll. Silence, a way to know. Silence, meditation, contemplation, call it what you will in the quietude of your soul. And when man has learned the quiescence of the soul, a thunder may roar, but man shall be undisturbed, for wrapped in the quietness of his inner self he shall hear no chaos around about or, as man calls it, the din on the without. Peace . . . within.

You have read, you have heard it stated that the Nazarene withdrew from the howling mob and his very own disciples, and he went up into the mountain and the desert place. What mountains? The mountain of silence. What desert place? That place which in consciousness was deserted of all chaos and all strife . . . not a physical desert, not a physical mountain . . . *Within.*

Bless You, Bless You, Bless You.

DISCERNING WHEAT FROM THE CHAFF

Our visits are for the purpose of enlightenment that you, dear ones, may be able to separate darkness from light; the unreal from the real, and truth from error.

You will ever remember, we of the Council as you, dear ones of the physical plane of life, we are all spiritual beings. There is but one difference. You, dear ones, yet remain in a physical habiliment. *We, as all who have experienced release from the physical habiliment, are unencumbered with the weight, the dross, and the limitation of the flesh.* Whether man is released from the flesh or yet a tenant of the flesh, *he is spiritual being.* And it is with interest . . . concern if you so care to call it . . . we return to enlighten man of the flesh . . . to enlighten man spiritually so.

When man of earth becomes spiritually enlightened there can be no darkness. And that which man accepts and refers to as problematic along his physical path shall in due season cease to be, for in God, that which man considers problematic is nonexistent. All confusion, all that which is problematic . . . so termed . . . is but mortal.

Therefore *strive, strive to rise in consciousness above the turmoil of mortal or physical confusion. Anger is a mortal attribute* and mind you dear hearts, we are released from the physical habiliment and know no anger, hate, nor comtempt.

Should it become necessary to speak with you, dear ones, or any of the many collaborators with whom we frequently visit; to speak in a manner which gives the appearance of that man calls stern, forceful, it is but because we shall be understood, and not have that which we speak misinterpreted in error.

We of the Council endeavor to make ourselves understood in acceptable language, making it unnecessary for those in the flesh with whom we visit to have need to refer to books of man-made knowledge, such as what man terms encyclopedias or dictionaries. It is our desire, our intended purpose, ever to lift and lead man on the mundane sphere of life.

We shall not, as you of earth would say, stand idly by and witness deception when it is within our power . . . and it is within our power to prevent it. "Evil communications corrupt good manners."

179

Dear hearts, sift the wheat from the chaff and feast upon the kernels of wheat. Let the chaff unto itself. Where there is spiritual illumination man is never in jeopardy of mortal deception. This is well to be remembered . . . forget it not.

And likewise, when he or she is living a dedicated life unto the Father's business, they shall never resort to the deception of subterfuge and that is to be remembered, please. We continue to lead you.

In our last visit with you dear ones, we reminded you that we desire to make no negative statements and we made no accusations deliberately. We endeavored to help you to separate the wheat of Truth from the chaff of deception. "Evil communications corrupt good manners." *Those who return from the vast expanse to lead and teach man here on the physical plane are not necromancers, soothsayers, nor charlatans and that is to be remembered, please.*

And necromancers, soothsayers, and charlatans of the flesh on earth can never prove to be an open door, nor a susceptible channel through which teachers of the vast expanse of life can pass through or *express* through . . . and that is to be remembered, please.

Listen within . . . quiescence is the open door.

Some, of the earth plane, call it meditation, concentration, and all manner of 'ations.' We of the Council say to you, *silence . . . there can be no commotion in silence. There, man of earth shall find but peace and comfort. Please, dear hearts, we have left with you dear ones, a pattern for silence. Music of any kind is agreeable and you have it. Desire silence, meditation, concentration.*

Should man of earth be in the leastwise disturbed by that which he has learned to call the chaos and commotion of his daily routine, what greater declaration of Truth may he listen to, and while listening to it silently repeat in agreement with it, the statements, "There is but one presence in the universe . . . God the good. I am now in the presence of pure being." If you are in agreement, in truth, with the statement that there is but one Presence in the Universe *God the Good,* it does not become necessary for you to deny the appearance of chaos, of turmoil. And when you have said in Truth, in Faith believing in Truth, there is but one Presence in the Universe . . . God the Good, you are giving recognition to only that Presence. And when in Truth, Faith believing in Truth, you will say, "I am now in the presence of pure being," you are recognizing your Oneness, your Sonship, your Christhood with the Living God. For remember, GOD IS PURE BEING. You spiritually are the image and likeness of God, therefore, spiritually, you are PURE BEING, dear hearts. And though a thousand times ten thousand darts and arrows of evil be directed in your path by the envy of mortal or carnal thinking, they can never become a part of you, and neither can they seek temporary or permanent lodgment at your dwelling place.

What are you declaring? What decree when you say, "I am now in the Presence of PURE BEING?" You are declaring, you are decreeing, please, your Spiritual Birthright with the Father. You are declaring that you have never left the Father's House, that nothing can take you from the Father's House. "I am now in the Presence of PURE BEING." And *NOW* expresses *Eternity and Eternity has been from the beginning of the beginning and shall be forever, world without end.*

THERE IS ONE PRESENCE IN THE UNIVERSE . . . . GOD THE GOOD. What would you dear ones make of the world you live in? What is your world? What would you have your world be? In Truth, it is the Universe of the Living God. For there is a vast difference in the recognition of man's world when he rises in spiritual consciousness. It is universal in the code of God and no longer measured or weighed my mundane events. Man or woman of the mundane spirit of life who yet indulges in mundane thinking, because of the reason that they have no greater teaching, lives in but a small world; a world of desire, as they make it.

When man understands what he is, his *world is Universal in God,* and no longer limited by the narrow confines of who he would be. We of the Council and all, who have experienced the release from physical habiliments no longer have mundane aspirations. And when it is that men of earth have aspirations to achieve, we recognize the truth that spiritual being in a physical habiliment has every right and privilege to physical or mundane achievements. But we admonish, seek first the kingdom of God, which is Universal. *In Truth, when physical achievement has been attained, it shall not perish, for it shall have been achieved through the fullness of the abundance of the universal good of God.*

There is but one power in the universe . . . God the good. I am now in the Presence of pure being. They who desired the achievements with Truth, and they shall not perish. Moth shall not devour them, rust shall not corrupt, neither shall thieves break through and steal.

There is but one entrance to the sheepfold. It is through a narrow door. There was a shepherd, as told in legend, and he became physically blind but yet remained devoted to his sheep, and he laid his body across the opening of the entrance to the sheepfold. He knew his sheep by numbers. When it came time for the sheep to enter the sheepfold, he raised his hand and he felt each sheep that entered, lest there perchance would be a wolf among them. It is the legend of the blind shepherd.

GOD IS NOT BLIND, dear hearts, yet the physical shepherd deprived of his physical vision loved his sheep and he said, "I shall count them as they enter." God loves his sheep and God is not blind, but it was the God Love in the heart's consciousness of the blind shepherd that willed to protect his sheep. He was a steward of the sheep and he was employed by a man whom he called his master. He was custodian of the flock, dear hearts.

You, dear ones, are not physically blind and we shall not permit spiritual blindness. We shall not permit spiritual blindness to interfere with the peace, quiet, and harmony of your Soul's consciousness. For when we are aware that mortal man, still feasting upon the five physical senses and its roots of deception, would seek to betray the God of all Life, do not fret, dear hearts; we shall not stand idly by and see he who has become blinded to Truth, and faithless to the sheep who have been entrusted into his or her care, deceive his sacred stewardship by mortal deception. We love you and we have compassion upon you and with the deceiver as well.

Blessed is it that *rebirth is an established, undeniable truth.* For it grants even the deceiver the blessed opportunity to return and labor zealously, lovingly, truthfully, in the field and vineyard of God.

Repeat silently and knowingly, meaningfully, please, when you say, "There is but one Presence in the Universe—God the Good." *Mean it . . . know it . . . accept it . . . receive it . . . appropriate it dear hearts. "I am now in the presence of pure being."* Mean it, know it. What other Presence can there be, and what other manner of being can you be with the decree, the declaration, the proclamation, *"I am now in the Presence of pure being?"* For remember, you are *spiritually the spark of the infinite. You are pure being. Thus you are declaring the truth of your identity with God-Pure Being.*

THE CHRIST LIGHT IS THE ACID TEST

In the seventh chapter in the Book of Ecclesiastes and the twenty-fifth verse and there you shall receive the key, if you will accept it and ponder upon it, the KEY TO THE STOREHOUSE OF INFINITE WISDOM. For you shall then be able to separate the *wheat of understanding from the chaff of mortal intellect.* It is well for man to study, but let man ask for divine wisdom enabling him to understand that which he studies.

Study becomes a folly, it becomes a madness to man's thinking when he does not divinely understand that which he studies. Unless it is divinely understood, it remains buried and hidden in the recesses of that which man refers to as occult. It remains hidden. When man of· earth in his objective thinking, indulges in destructive criticism, he passes the indulgence of his objective thinking, to the subjective chamber and can expect no other reflection from the subjective other than that which he has therein implanted. It hinders spiritual growth.

Just recently we spoke to you dear ones relative to objective thinking, subjective memory and the Superconscious or Godmind and we used the term, "The spirit is willing but the flesh is weak." When the king sits upon his throne and rules his subjects, he expects his subjects to be obedient to his rule. And when that which the subjective mind has received and returns to the objective thinking, it is as the king expects . . . in fact demands . . . that the objective thinking become obedient to his command. And when the objective thinking becomes obedient to the subjective and confusion arises along the life's path of man because of that which the subjective mind has commanded, man then is prone to blame his neighbor and make accusations in every manner and direction, but that which he has created for himself. But the superconscious mind or Godmind continues to knock upon the door.

The Christ Mind says, "Let me in, let me help you." And the door upon which the Godmind, the Christmind knocks, that door has no latch upon the outside, it must be opened from the inside, that the Godmind or the Christmind might manifest. How shall you open it? Read the twenty-fifth verse of the seventh chapter of Ecclesiastes, dear hearts. How shall man proceed? When he receives the spiritual beauty, the spiritual significance of the verse, he shall proceed with right thinking in his conscious or objective mind. Thus the thoughts of beauty, eradicating all thoughts of antagonism, debate, theory, and beholding in desire to become conscious of his oneness with God. He shall then eradicate all confusion from the subjective mind and fill it with the desire for spiritual illumination, God illumination, Christ illumination.

All the knowledge that he has acquired, he shall bathe with the desire for spiritual illumination. Then knowledge shall become wisdom. Wisdom shall become understanding. Godmind, Christmind shall be free to manifest. Doubt shall fly out of the door and the window, antagonism shall cease to be and man shall no longer live in a state of mental madness. For as the verse stated, "He shall have separated himself from the folly, the foolishness of madness.

Education, yes, by all means, what would be the advantage of we of the council to speak with you dear ones, or with any of the many collaborators with whom we have the blessed privilege of visiting, if education was unnecessary. Listen to the wisdom of Solomon when he said, "Get wisdom, get understanding, and forget it not. Wisdom is the principle thing and with all thy getting, get understanding."

Acquired knowledge can become wisdom when it is spiritually understood and because of spiritual understanding of that acquired knowledge, it became spiritually applied. *That is seeking the Christ along the Path of Regeneration. Mortal intellect can deceive, dear hearts. But when it is placed in the presence of the great white light of the Christ and tarnishes not, nor disintegrates, that knowledge then becomes wisdom.*

Man of earth refers to putting certain objects, certain people, if you please, to what he calls the acid test, *the Christ light is the acid test of that which is acquired through the channel of mortal intellect.* The twenty-fifth verse in the seventh chapter of Ecclesiates, "I applied my heart to seek and to search . . . I applied my heart." Bless you a thousand times ten thousand if you have listened attentively, without an antagonistic thought. Antagonism is the first step to rejection, dear hearts. If you have listened patiently with a receptive desire, from memories pages you shall recall the words we have left with you. We love you, and we have promised you that we would not stand idly by and see you deceived or misled, and that is not only referring to the deception and misleading of mortals as you understand them, it is referring to your own thinking.

Be not deceived, "Evil communication, corrupt good manners."

Bless You, Bless You, Bless You.

DIVINE INTELLIGENCE

Greetings;

We speak the word of Life, the word of Light, the word of Pure Being to those whose physical temples are in need of peace, power, health and every good portion of God's abundant spiritual riches. We speak the word that quickens, illumines and heals. You are now in the presence of Pure Being. You are conscious of the healing, cleansing regeneration power of Spirit, renewing your mind and body. Arise, come forth and live. In the name of the Living Christ of God. So be it.

The collaborator who fully surrenders in Love, without fear, with but one desire to serve God and his fellowman in service of God, becomes a channel of expression for disincarnate teachers, who desire to share the message of Light, Life and Truth. It is unnecessary for the collaborator to possess or to have ever possessed intellectual knowledge.

The greater the desire in the collaborator's conscious mind or objective thinking in Truth, the greater is the opportunity for the wisdom and intelligence of the disincarnate teachers to express through that which man of earth knows as the subconscious or subjective channel.

Willingness because of devoted desire in the conscious thinking of the collaborator, renders the subjective channel, so called, devoid of any intellectual, and may we use the word . . . clutter. Disembodied teachers do not depend upon any knowledge whatsoever accumulated by the collaborator. The less the collaborator has delved into intellectual knowledge the greater the opportunity for the disembodied teachers to bring the message of Truth.

To use the vernacular of the mundane sphere, there is no mortal or intellectual training necessary on the part of the collaborator. All that the disincarnate teacher desire is willingness through full surrender in love. Mortal intellect can become an obstacle, but temporarily so. When the mundane collaborator retires to the silent chamber, he or she in retiring therein with a fervent desire to serve, closes all known physical avenues to intellectual knowledge.

We of the council do not attempt to eulogize in the least wise anyone of the collaborators whose physical temple we are privileged to use. *Residing in the physical habiliment dwells the Spirit of God, as you, the Spirit of God, inhabits or dwells in your physical habiliments.* Every kindness, every comfort you bestow upon a physical habiliment, you bestow upon Spirit. While in your mortal reckoning, or objective thinking, because of physically beholding the physical habiliment, you have formulated the thought . . . idea, that. *That* which you have rendered, has but been to a physical being, *but it has been to God.*

And here, may we please clarify a statement of the Nazarene which has been grossly misunderstood because of misinterpretation, when he said, "Inasmuch as ye do this unto the least of these, my brethren, ye do it also unto me." And *that was the Christ of God speaking through the physical habiliment of the mortal Jesus.* THE CHRIST SPOKE. Therefore, every kindness, be it thought, word or deed which man renders unto his fellowman, when in consciousness he becomes aware that his kindness is rendered unto God and not just to mortal man. And when that kindness is rendered and when the collaborator who zealously desires to serve his fellowman in service rendered to God, as he enters the chamber of silence, there is but one desire, that his life, so to speak, shall be a life of service, unselfishly rendered.

The adept collaborator is not desirous of the right hand revealing to the left hand. Nor is the adept collaborator seeking the ovations and plaudits on the street corners, as it were, of men. Humility is the path. Many are they who are willing, willing to live mortally so unnoticed and satisfied with, if it needs must be with the crumbs that fall from the table of those who have the loaf upon the table.

This is not necessary, but if it needs be, the avowed, the adept collaborator is willing to endure that, if called upon to so do. There is an abundance, dear hearts. Abundance is Spiritual. It cannot perish, for the reason that the Creator of abundance cannot perish. And woe betide unto the man or woman of earth, who in your mundane vernacular takes undue advantage of any kindness, in thought, word, deed or action, that you, dear hearts, or anyone else of the mundane sphere renders. Woe betide unto that individual for remember, life is endless. And therefore the Nazarene likewise spoke in Truth when he said, "Forgive us our debtors as we forgive our debtors."

In your Holy Writ you will read a narrative in this wise, "There was a man who owed a sum of money to his master, and he went unto his master when the sum of money was due for payment, and the master dealt kindly with him and demanded not payment of the money. He said, "Go forth, my son and worry not." And the man went forth and while traveling along the road he met a man who owed him a sum of money. He had forgotten how the master had dealt with him and he demanded of the man the payment of the money and placed him in bondage until the debt was paid. The news of that act came to the master who had freed the one his debt. The master sent for that man and he said to him, "Why have you dealt unkindly with your fellowman and placed him in bondage, until he has paid you? Were you in like manner dealt with?" And the master placed him in bondage.

Now this is a story the Nazarene related. Who masters who? Who is the master? Is not each man a master unto himself? How does man use mastery . . . graciously or ungraciously? Unto he, who uses it graciously, graciousness is the experience. Unto he or she, who uses mastery ungraciously, ungraciousness is his reward.

In the Ancient Aramaic Writ, this statement was made, *"I am the center of the Universe, from me all things radiate, unto me all things gravitate."* And the early translators placed it to read in this wise, "As ye sow, so shall ye reap." Each lesson, as we have endeavored to leave these lessons with you dear heart, do not bear any semblance of any record which Frater Achad or any other collaborator has recorded in the subjective mind, because of acquired intellectual knowledge. Each lesson has come to you through THE CHANNEL OF DIVINE INTELLIGENCE. As you refer to previous lessons we have left with you, you shall receive enlightenment as to intellect and intelligence.

Now, remember, man is Spirit. There is but One Spirit and that is the Spirit of God, God is not a Spirit, God is Spirit. And therefore man, his image and likeness is Spirit, not a Spirit. Man is One in the oneness of God. All intelligence is of God. It is Divine. Each teacher who passes the lesson of Truth, Light, Life and Love, has at some time or other, as you understand the term, travelled the physical path

in the physical habiliment, that he may have experienced the blessedness of Divine Intelligence. Are you experiencing it, dear hearts? Is
life's path a wee mite sweeter to you, physically so?

When circumstances, conditions, bring about experiences along
your life's path, have you gained a spiritual understanding wherewith
you may deal with the experience? Do you still walk on a darkened
path, or is your path brighter? Are you experiencing greater happiness or are you still, in your thinking, inclined to experience seasons
of remorse and sorrow?

What is Divine Intelligence doing for you? Are you separating the
wheat from the chaff? Are you able to distinguish the wheat from the
tares? Are you able in truth to say, "All man . . . One in Spirit . . .
and in Truth . . . in God." And in so beholding man, do you yet
have fear of what he, because of his lack of understanding of his
Oneness with God, may do to you mortally so?

Unregenerated man cannot injure you. You need have no fear of
unregenerate man, when you do not behold him unregenerated.
When you look beyond his unregenerated state and behold him . . .
the image and likeness of God, as *You* are the image and likeness of
God, you are beholding man in his Pure Estate. And when you hold
in consciousness, man in his Pure Estate, there can be no harm befall
you.

Remember the little story of Buddha we have related to you.
Buddha did not accept the gift, do you remember? He beheld the one
who would vilify him and persecute him, he beheld that one, the
image and likeness of God. He did not accept the mortal accusations.
Likewise, have we not frequently stated, please, "Render unto Caesar
that which is Caesar's and unto God that which is God's."

And, when man would seek, as you would say, to take advantage
of you, behold not his mortal limitation. For if you do, in your
consciousness, you are accepting his mortal limitations. Buddha did
not accept. What are you to behold and accept? What you accept,
needs to be appropriated. Therefore, Buddha did not accept and there
was naught for Buddha to appropriate. He said, "You are my brother.
I am your brother." Yes, yes, dear hearts. Man but becomes a part of
that which he beholds. When man beholds the beauty of Spirit,
which is Divine Intelligence made manifest, that he appropriates.

May we use this term to a very good advantage. Do not fear . . . do not doubt . . . doubt and fear are handmaidens.

Would you say to we of the Council, "How am I to know?" May we answer you in this wise. "What are your intentions with your fellowman when you are dealing with them?" How do you expect from the manner in which you conduct yourself with your fellowman, that your fellowman shall accept you. That is the answer.

Remember, the master released the one who felt an indebtedness to him and sent him forth. But the one who was released did not deal as kindly with the one whom he held in bondage for the debt that, that one owed him. Mastery . . . what had he mastered? What mastered him?

Bless you, dear hearts, and this lesson, call it a lesson if you will, feel free to share wherever and whenever the opportunity for sharing presents itself. We have left it with you, dear ones, that it may bring Light, Life, Freedom to he or she who hears it. Share it, dear hearts, share it. Bless you.

ENTERING THE SILENCE INTO THE PRESENCE OF PURE BEING

Why does man of earth seek the silence? What difference is there in that which man calls the silence than that mental state with which he is familiar in his ordinary frame of thinking? With what portion of the brain does man do his thinking? Is it with the objective portion of the brain? And how come that man has a memory? Where is the seat of memory? How does man proceed to enter that state of mental quiescence known as the silence? Can man enter the chamber of silence and continue to be absorbed in all the confusing and conflicting thoughts of the mortal?

What part of that, which man calls silence, does man remain aware of? Of what interest is the silence to man? As man becomes interested in exploring the chambers of silence, the subjective or memory seat becomes permeated with just that which man desires to remain aware of.

Man shall be sincere in entering the chamber of silence, for in the chamber of silence, *it is there that man makes contact with that which is unknown to mortal thinking.* It is in the chamber of silence that the formless takes form. It is as that which man refers to as the beginning. It is the creative seat and *man cannot enter the silence if man is at variance with himself, argumentative, debative, or critical with himself or his fellowman* while in the mortal or objective chamber.

All arguments, all debates, all destructive criticism of the mortal, shall be eradicated before any attempt is made to enter the chamber of silence. If there were a heavy snow drift in front of your door it would be much easier for you to leave your house if the snow drift were cleared away. It would not be nearly as difficult as wading through the snow. Therefore, he or she who refrains from argument or debate or destructive criticism about themselves or their fellowman is expediently wise. For man cannot enter the silence without moving, so to speak, through the mortal or objective channel.

Man's thinking takes place in the objective chamber. Does man then objectify the chamber of silence before he can enter into it?

192

And, in all manner of conversation which causes conflict in man's thinking, is engaged in before he proceeds to enter the chamber of silence; it is as the snow drift before the door of his house. Therefore, it is expediently wise for man to begin to clear away the drift of all erroneous or contrary thinking and become quiet before he proceeds to enter the chamber of silence.

Man shall never find conflict in the chamber of silence. Conflict is only found in man's mortal thinking. THE CHAMBER OF SI-LENCE IS MAN'S DIVINE SELF. IT IS THERE THAT MAN MEETS MAN'S GOD. And when man earnestly enters the chamber of silence, his experience there becomes a subjective picture, and man then remains subject to reflections from the subjective chamber of that which he experiences in the chamber of silence.

When man is meditating and seemingly unresponsive to the conversation of those about him, it is unwise for he or she who is in meditation, to be disturbed by inquisitive questioning for there is a sacred reverie in silence. The silence chamber never reflects that which is problematic, for it is free of all manner of confusion, and it is unkind for neighbor, friend, or relative to disturb he or she who is in the depths of silent reverie. Having no fear of seeing your loved ones in silent meditation, for when that is taking place they are in the presence of pure being.

When man emerges from the depths of the silent chamber, quietly and without being disturbed, it is then that the imprint is made upon the subjective records. *Silence then continues its action, and when man then is in need of that which he calls comfort, solace, from the memory of the subjective chamber, comes the recorded message, that has been experienced in the chamber of silence.*

How well does man remember all other events of his thinking? Is it therefore not logical that he shall remember the peace and the beauty of his experience in silence. For nothing is ever lost, dear hearts, and when in silence man has resigned his all of everything to PURE BEING, let him then not in mortal thinking, become destructive through suspicious and antagonistic thought of circumstances, conditions, which arise because of that which he feels is unbecoming by his fellowman.

The Nazarene was expediently wise when he said, "Bless those

who persecute you and revile and say all manner of evil against you,"
for in so doing, dear hearts, you are heaping coals of the purifying fire
upon them. But when man becomes displeased by that which he calls
the conduct of his fellowman, he is but becoming a part of that which
displeased him. But when he blesses his fellowman and in the Presence of Pure Being, prays with his fellowman, though his fellowman
may be wholly unaware of it, consciously so, yet he who prays for his
fellowman is elevating his fellowman in the Presence of Pure Being.

You may say it is well for we of the Council so to speak because we
are no longer a part of the confusion of the mundane sphere of Life.
As tenants of physical habiliments, we grant you, we are no longer a
part of mundane confusion, but we are concerned with those who are,
and if there is restitution to be made, which there is, then it becomes
necessary that man of earth be taught how that restitution is to be
made. If it were impossible for restitution to come into manifestation,
then there would be no necessity to teach the lesson of becoming a
part of Pure Being.

The statement is Truth, "As a man thinketh in his heart, so is he."
And as long as man of earth accepts all that of confusion which he
beholds in his fellowman and conjures it in his heart's consciousness,
he shall never be any greater than the one whom he criticizes. For
you will be mindful of the words of an age-old mystic when he said,
and we are speaking of Apostle Paul. And the Apostle Paul said, and
continues to say, "man becomes a part of that which he beholds," and
remember the story of the narrative of the "beam and the mote."

*It is of no avail for man to enter the chamber of Silence, unless he
becomes a part of that which he finds in the chamber of silence.* The
man who is called wicked is not beyond redemption, and should your
fellowman give the appearance of wickedness, behold him in the
Presence of Pure Being for remember and never forget, he is a
spiritual entity, and not just a physical being. Therefore, blessing him
with the Presence of Pure Being, the appearance of wickedness is
overcome.

But will you say to we of the Council, "How shall we do this when
it interferes with our daily progress?" You are seeking progress are
you not? AND TRUE PROGRESS COMES OF SPIRITUAL
GROWTH. All there is of growth has its origin in the spiritual

womb of God. For remember, in the beginning was the word, and the word became flesh.

What word is man of earth to hold in silence? What word is man to speak in an audible manner concerning the seeming undoing of his fellowman? . . . A creative one, or a destructive word? Since the word becomes flesh, then it behooves man of earth to think and speak constructively . . . that is, abiding by the Christ Principle of Life and Life is Divine substance and becomes physically manifest as man expresses it first in his thinking.

Before a word can be spoken audibly, it must be first formulated in thought or thinking. Every act and deed is the outward expression of man's thinking and cannot be otherwise. Therefore, that which is contrary to divine law begets all that which is contrary to divine law. And because man has been unschooled, improperly taught, man finds himself in that which man calls a state of confusion.

There is no confusion in God. Confusion is but mortal. Hate is the absence of love and love is the absence of hate.

Let man's handclasp be real, genuine. When man, in his thinking says, "I Love you," let it be genuine, let it be real and let the word hate be unmentioned, unthought of, ever in idle conversation. For remember, man ever becomes a part of that which he beholds, even though he but beholds it in his thinking.

Let man become subjective to that which is spiritual . . . ever . . . and the snowdrift shall melt and pass away. And man shall walk a path of freedom. For remember, though there be a million physical habiliments, there is but one Presence, the Presence of God and God Presence is ever desirous of manifesting. *Man's thinking is the channel through which God expresses and man's evil thinking against himself and his fellowman retards the manifestation of God, which is pure being.*

How often do we of the Council hear man say, "I wonder if it will work . . . I wonder if it is right . . . I wonder if it is fair . . . I wonder if it is worth while." And that is what they will receive, continued wonderment, wonderment, wonderment. There is no wonderment in God. There is no doubt in Pure Being . . . Pure, Pure Being is devoid of doubt. All doubt exists in man's mortal thinking.

Now then when you approach the avenue of silence . . . clear away all the snowbanks of doubt before opening the door to the chamber of silence, erase all that of mortal confusion, remove the sandals from your feet, as it were, and enter the Temple of Silence.

The more often you enter without confusion, though you may be ever so confused before you enter, leave it on the soles of your sandals and leave your sandals on the outside.

Do not take doubt with you in the chamber of silence and should you find your loved ones wrapped in the reverie of silence in the chamber of silence and its awe, disturb them not, for they may have entered for peace of mind.

Peace . . . Peace . . . Peace.

INDEX

A

Absolution, 78

Abundance, 31, 33, 55, 110, 130, 157, 187; cannot perish, 188; God's, 122, 188; I Am, 50; infinite, 103; life, 85, 155; multiplied, 122; receiving, 37; spiritual, 47, 188; universal good, 182

Accepting, 24, 84, 93, 139, 142

Achievements, 127, 181, 182

Acorn, 38

Acid tests, 184, 185

Acts, 24, 66, 195

Action, 132, 172, 177

Adam, 133, 134

Adoration, 85

Adversity, 17, 20, 42, 43, 97, 116, 169, 176

Advocates, 121

Agreement, 42, 92

Akasic record, 39, 74, 79, 81

Alabaster box, 166

Altar, 35, 39, 44, 60, 64, 113, 147, 154, 172

Ambassador of God, 81, 93, 150, 151

Ambition, 126, 127, 128

Amenhotep of Egypt, 59

Ancient age teachers, 59

Ancient Aramaic writ, 189

Ancient Mystical White Brotherhood (see Council of), 28, 150; never commands, 36, 39; unseen, 150

Angels, 167, 168, 169

Angelic, hosts, 137

Anxiety, 101

Apostle Paul, 24, 25, 45, 46, 48, 72, 80, 88, 90, 92, 114, 116, 117, 164, 166, 194

Apron, 38, 136

Appearance, 16; deceived, 75; feeble, 143; given over, 75; lack, 62; outer, 62, 164; physical error, 124; positive, 62

Apple, 17, 31, 77, 96, 105

Appropriate, 84, 139, 140, 190

Aramaic translations, 41, 47

Aramathustra, 59

Arcadia, 107

Architect of Universe, 145

Arms, 14

Ascending, 88, 89, 107, 128, 138

Asking, 89, 95, 160

Asp, 135, 136

Aspiration, 21

Astral Body, 28

Astral flight, 28

Astral plane of life, 25

Astral shell, 24, 25

Atheist, 38

Atom, 158

Atonement, 77

Attraction, 25, 168

Attributes of mortals, 121, 127, 192

A U M, 59

Aura, 26, 39, 74, 91

B

Bag, 77

Bacon, Sir Francis, 89

Banker, 35

Battles of life, 108

Beam in eye, 176

Beatitudes, 157

Beauty, 22, 46, 137, 148, 154, 156, 185

Believe, 155

Betrayer, 95

Benediction of love, 33

Bible or Holy Writ—text book of life, 39, 41, 81, 103, 124, 135, 166, 173, 189

Birthright, 19, 77, 93, 125, 147, 148, 181

Blasphemy, 47, 49, 99, 105, 155

Blessing, 19, 23, 34, 35, 38, 123, 162, 168, 169; bestowed, 82; circum-

Conception, mortal, 36; immaculate, 91, 93
Concern spiritual, 37
Condemnation, 23, 24, 60, 63, 90, 105, 109, 114, 147
Conduct, 86
Confession of faith, 87, 89
Confidence, 159
Confucius, 59, 112
Confused, 14
Confusion, 21, 37, 43, 59, 60, 65, 88, 103, 104, 105, 125, 126, 128, 140, 144, 164, 167, 170, 186, 194, 195; not of God, 15, 71, 99, 114, 116, 124, 164, 193, 196
Conquest, 13
Conscience, 120, 147, 148
Consciousness, 18, 45, 74, 133; ascending, 65, 70, 87, 128, 179; beholding new, 49, 114, 120, 148; buried riches, 173, 177; Christ, 45, 51, 85, 95, 114, 165; confinement in, 168; conjured criticism, 194; disobedient to God, 121; discards and chooses, 117, 118, 122, 147, 148; hearts, 36, 106, 155, 164; in bondage, 96, 104; no fear, 136; proper reference to God, 59; regeneration, 43, 51, 72, 87, 93, 187; soul's 30, 38, 113, 144, 151, 182; table in, 31, 32, 173, 181; surrender, 43, 87; where God is, 67, 111, 145, 150, 155, 166, 177, 181, 182
Contempt, 66, 78
Corn, 96
Cosmos, eternal, 74
Council, of White Brotherhood, 18, 28, 95, 111, 112, 115, 123, 163, 167, 179, 181, 185, 190, 194, 195; chooses from all walks, 75; fellowship, 53; in attendance, 39; labor, 100; never comamnds, 165; never eulogizes, 188; no aspirations, 181; not deceived by appearances, 75; unseen, 79, 177
Counterclock, in digression, 88, 89
Courage, 30, 135, 152
Court, 32
Covetousness, 82
Creation—never ceased, 80, 82, 83, 136, 143, 144, 145, 147, 153, 154, 157, 158, 168, 169, 175, 184, 189, 192, 195

Creative power of God, 33, 49, 93
Creator, 22, 58, 59
Credit, 37
Creed, 68, 109, 110, 111, 154
Criticism, 75, 115, 192
Crooked paths, 54
Cross, 14, 16, 132, 151, 153
Cross roads, 140
Crown thorn, 107
Crucifixion of body, 45, 47, 85; of 5 senses, 95
Crucify, 14, 16
Cup, 33, 84, 111, 118, 152, 153, 155

D

Day, 18, 86, 145, 148, 159, 162, 171
Darkness, 125, 143, 144, 145, 147, 148, 165, 179, 190
Daughter, 12
Deaf, 11
Death, 11, 14, 17, 18, 21, 35, 44, 45, 47, 66, 141, 166, 172, 174; willed, 100
Debased, 15
Debts or debtors, 86, 88, 160, 188, 189, 191; redeemed, 39, 40, 41, 47, 78
Deceived, 78
Deceiving or deception, 22, 76, 77, 129, 130, 132, 137, 172, 177, 180, 186; never necessary, 72; returns to work, 182; the thief, 82
Decision, 127
Decree, 11, 70
Dedication, 92, 122, 162; life, 120, 160, 180
Deed, 24, 25, 88, 164, 195
Defeat, 36
Degradation, 23
Delineation, 89
Denominations, 68, 109
Denial of self, 81
Desecrated love destroys, 131
Desert places, 178
Derelict of society, 122
Desires, bring rebirth, 69, 88, 104, 105, 163, 168, 186; earnestly, 27, 72, 104, 111; for experiences, 19, 36, 82, 119, 136; for good, 25, 81, 187; mortal, 11, 15, 18, 26, 32, 49, 74, 75, 80, 81, 87, 103, 109, 118, 126, 130, 133, 136, 143, 151, 157, 160, 168, 181; to serve God, 28,